C000133076

The Routledge Guidebook to Berkeley's *Three Dialogues*

The Routledge Guidebook to Berkeley's Three Dialogues is an engaging introduction to the last of a trio of works that cemented Berkeley's position as one of the truly great philosophers of the western canon. Berkeley's distinctive idealist philosophy has been a challenge and inspiration for thinkers ever since.

Written for readers approaching this seminal work for the first time, this book:

- provides the philosophical context in which *Three Dialogues* was written;
- critically discusses the arguments in each of the *Three Dialogues*; and
- examines some of the principal disputes concerning the interpretation of his work.

The Routledge Guidebook to Berkeley's Three Dialogues offers a clear and comprehensive guide to this ground-breaking volume and includes further reading sections at the end of each chapter. This is essential reading for anyone who wants to understand this influential work.

Stefan Storrie has published extensively on early modern philosophy, and Berkeley in particular. He is the editor of *Berkeley's Three Dialogues: New Essays* (2018) and, with Ezio Di Nucci, *1984 and Philosophy* (2018).

THE ROUTLEDGE GUIDES TO THE GREAT BOOKS

A full list of titles in this series can be found at https://www.routledge.com/The-Routledge-Guides-to-the-Great-Books/book-series/RGGB

The Routledge Guides to the Great Books

The Routledge Guidebook to Berkeley's *Three Dialogues*

Stefan Storrie

Routledge
Taylor & Francis Group

LONDON AND NEW YORK

First published 2019
by Routledge
2 Park Square, Milton Park, Abingdon, Oxon OX14 4RN

and by Routledge
52 Vanderbilt Avenue, New York, NY 10017

Routledge is an imprint of the Taylor & Francis Group, an informa business

British Library Cataloguing-in-Publication Data
A catalogue record for this book is available from the British Library

Library of Congress Cataloging-in-Publication Data
A catalog record has been requested for this book

ISBN: 978-1-138-69404-0 (hbk)
ISBN: 978-1-138-69405-7 (pbk)
ISBN: 978-0-429-39930-5 (ebk)

Typeset in Times New Roman
by Swales & Willis Ltd, Exeter, Devon, UK

MIX
Paper from
responsible sources
FSC
www.fsc.org FSC® C013056

Printed and bound in Great Britain by
TJ International Ltd, Padstow, Cornwall

For my parents

CONTENTS

Acknowledgements

I would like to thank David Berman, who was first my teacher and then colleague at Trinity College Dublin. I have benefited greatly over the years from our discussions of all things Berkeley. I would also like to thank all my students over the years who participated in my "Great Texts: Berkeley's *Three Dialogues*" seminar at Trinity College Dublin. Finally, I would like to thank Peter Larsen for his assiduous reading of the draft of this book. His many recommendations made the manuscript more readable and philosophically sharper.

ABBREVIATIONS

Alciphron = Berkeley, George. *Alciphron: Or, the Minute Philosopher*. In *The Works of George Berkeley, Bishop of Cloyne*. Ed. A. A. Luce and T. E. Jessop, 9 vols (Edinburgh and London: Thomas Nelson, 1948–57), vol. 3, pp. 1–329.

AT = *Œuvres de Descartes*. Ed. Charles Adam and Paul Tannery, 11 vols. (Paris: J. Vrin, 1996).

CSM = *The Philosophical Writings of Descartes*. Ed. John Cottingham, Robert Stoothoff, Dugald Murdoch and Anthony Kenny, 3 vols (Cambridge: Cambridge University Press, 1985–91).

Essay = Locke, John. *An Essay concerning Human Understanding*. Ed. Peter. H. Nidditch (Oxford: Clarendon Press, 1975).

New Theory = Berkeley, George. *An Essay toward a New Theory of Vision*. In *The Works of George Berkeley, Bishop of Cloyne*. Ed. A. A. Luce and T. E. Jessop, 9 vols (Edinburgh and London: Thomas Nelson, 1948–57), vol. 1, pp. 161–241.

Notebooks = Berkeley, George. *Notebooks*. In *The Works of George Berkeley, Bishop of Cloyne*. Ed. A. A. Luce and T. E. Jessop, 9 vols (Edinburgh and London: Thomas Nelson, 1948–57), vol. 1, pp. 1–139.

Principles = Berkeley, George. *A Treatise concerning the Principles of Human Knowledge*. In *The Works of George Berkeley, Bishop of Cloyne*. Ed. A. A. Luce and T. E. Jessop, 9 vols (Edinburgh and London: Thomas Nelson, 1948–57), vol. 2, pp. 19–145; and in *Philosophical Writings*. Ed. D. M. Clarke (Cambridge: Cambridge University Press, 2008), pp. 67–149. Reference to section number in *Works*.

Search = Malebranche, Nicolas. *The Search after Truth*. Tr. Thomas Lennon and Paul Olscamp (Columbus: Ohio State University Press, 1980).

Siris = *Siris: A Chain of Philosophical Reflexions and Inquiries concerning the Virtues of Tar Water*. In *The Works of George Berkeley, Bishop of Cloyne*. Ed. A. A. Luce and T. E. Jessop, 9 vols (Edinburgh and London: Thomas Nelson, 1948–57), vol. 5, 1–163. Reference to section number in *Works*.

Three Dialogues = Berkeley, George. *Three Dialogues between Hylas and Philonous*. In *The Works of George Berkeley, Bishop of Cloyne*. Ed. A. A. Luce and T. E. Jessop, 9 vols (Edinburgh and London: Thomas Nelson, 1948–57), vol. 2, pp. 147–263.

1

THE CONTEXT OF BERKELEY'S
THREE DIALOGUES

I am young, I am an upstart, I am a pretender, I am vain, very
well. [. . .] But one thing I know I am not guilty of. I do not pin
my faith on the sleeve of any great man. I act not out of prejudice
& prepossession. I do not adhere to any opinion because it is
an old one, a receiv'd one, a fashionable one, or one that I have
spent much time in the study and cultivation of.

Notebooks §465

George Berkeley (1685–1753) was born near Kilkenny in Ireland
and, like most people, he was born into turbulent times. Europe,
Britain and Ireland had entered into the modern period both intel-
lectually and politically. The Stuart period (1603–1714) saw Britain
moving towards a modern form of society through a series of conflicts resulting from a complex set of related oppositions within
society. Central issues were: the respective legal and moral rights
and obligations of king and of parliament, the religious divide
between Protestants and Catholics, and the political opposition of
the parliamentary groupings of Whig (very broadly liberal) and

Tory (very broadly conservative). Berkeley embodied many of the conflicts and oppositions at the time, leading these developments and reshaping them into his own distinctive outlook and aims.

Philosophically, his major influences (at least in his early years) were John Locke and Nicolas Malebranche. They were leaders of what is commonly seen as the opposing outlooks of empiricism and rationalism. Berkeley pushed some of their central tenets to their ultimate conclusion, often going further than they could imagine. With Locke, he sought to centre the discussion of our knowledge of the world on experiential evidence, clarify the relation between language and perception, and work out the view that everything that exists is particular. At the same time, like Malebranche, Berkeley's philosophical project sees God at the centre of his system, and also denies the causal efficacy of any physical object in the natural world. He was of English Protestant descent, yet he was born in Ireland and identified closely with the country and its people – as a philosopher, as a social activist and economist, and later as a bishop. This chapter will present a brief sketch of these contexts, beginning with a historical background of the political and religious setting, then moving on to Berkeley's life, and then to the philosophical context.

HISTORICAL BACKGROUND

The first Stuart to rule Great Britain was James I (1566–1625). He worked mainly for achieving unity between England and Scotland, and at the same time began the plantation of Ulster (the north-eastern province of the island of Ireland), turning Ireland into an early colonial experiment. His son, Charles I (1600–49), had an authoritarian understanding of his royal powers, which led to two civil wars and eventually to regicide. Berkeley's father's family were royal supporters and it is believed that they suffered for their loyalty. The parliamentary rule that replaced the Crown was not equipped to govern the country and the second in command of the New Model Army, Oliver Cromwell (who was also one of the signatories of Charles' death warrant), was invited to lead the country as Lord Protector of the Commonwealth. The royalists regrouped in Ireland and Cromwell responded by leading a parliamentary invasion there in 1649–50. The campaign was brief and unusually brutal, with several thousand civilians massacred in Drogheda and in

Wexford. The outcome of this conflict was the cementation of Ireland as a poor, subservient British colony. The Act for the Settlement of Ireland (1652) led to all the land owned by Catholics being confiscated and given to Scottish and English Protestant settlers, parliament's financial creditors and parliamentary soldiers. The public practice of Catholicism was banned.

Shortly after Cromwell's death (1658) Charles II was restored as king. The Berkeley family's fortunes now changed and George's grandfather was rewarded for his loyalty to the Crown. He settled in the Kilkenny area as a gentleman farmer and also received a good income as tax collector, a position later held by George's father William. Berkeley's mother is thought to have been Elizabeth née Southerne, who was from a Dublin family. During the reign of Charles II political differences in British society crystallized into two opposing parties, 'Tory' and 'Whig'. The Tories supported the principle of divine right monarchy and insisted that civil authority derived directly from God. According to this logic, rebellion was never permissible and therefore the doctrine of 'passive obedience' was adhered to. They were also typically strongly aligned to 'high church' Anglicanism, which emphasized formality and resistance to modernization, bringing them closer to Catholicism and further away from evangelism. The Whigs, by contrast, held that civil authority derived from the people and that a ruler who ceased to govern for the public good betrayed the trust reposed in him and therefore could, by right, be resisted. The theoretical framework for the Whig position was worked out by John Locke in his *Two Treatises of Government* (1690). Whigs typically adhered to 'low church' Anglicanism, which strove for a liberalization and simplification of church structure and identified with a strongly Protestant ethos.

The year Berkeley was born Charles II died and the King's brother James II succeeded him. James had converted to Catholicism and sought to ensure the permanent legal toleration of Catholicism in England. In striving for this goal he stretched his royal prerogative to its limits, displaying many of the same authoritarian tendencies as his father Charles I. The same year Louis XIV revoked the Edict of Nantes, which guaranteed the religious freedom and legal equality of France's one million Protestants (Huguenots). Over the next three years 50,000–80,000 Huguenots fled to England with shocking stories of their suffering.

The Anglican hierarchy accepted James' Catholic-friendly policies as long as his only possible successors were his two Protestant daughters. Matters drastically changed when Queen Mary gave birth to a Roman Catholic son and heir in 1688. Later that year seven Protestant noblemen invited William of Orange (James' nephew and the husband of his daughter Mary) to invade England, an event known as the 'Glorious Revolution'. After some fighting in England, James fled and in 1689 the crown was offered jointly to William III and Mary II (yes, they were spouses, first cousins and joint rulers of Britain). Military attention now turned to Ireland. The Irish Catholic Tyrconnell had raised a large army and controlled most of Ireland, with the exception of the Protestant strongholds in Ulster. He was joined by James II who brought troops from France. William thought it necessary to intervene and landed with a large number of English, Danish, Dutch and French Huguenots. For a short time, Ireland became the theatre for a Europe-wide war. William won the decisive battle of the Boyne in 1690 and by 1691 he had achieved a complete victory. However, the political movement in support of James II and his heirs, known as 'Jacobitism' continued well into the 1700s, with strongholds in Ireland, the Scottish Highlands, as well as in parts of Wales and England. Berkeley published a work on moral and political philosophy in 1712 with the title *Passive Obedience*. It appeared to many contemporary observers to take a High Tory position verging on Jacobitism. Berkeley strenuously denied this and used all political capital available to him to wash that label off. Nevertheless, the publication hindered his advancement in the Church for many years and speculation about the political import of the work has been hotly contested from Berkeley's own lifetime to the present (see Berman 1986 and Ross 2005).

The next 25 years were characterized by continent-wide war, the Nine Years War (1689–97) and the War of the Spanish Succession (1702–13), with shifting alliances which centred on Protestant England aiming to contain Catholic France, the continent's true military superpower. Mary II died in 1694 and William ruled alone until his death in 1702. As William and Mary had no children, they were succeeded by Anne (James II's daughter, William's cousin and Mary's sister), a staunch Protestant who continued William's struggle with France. While the war ended in a stalemate, the Treaties of Utrecht (March and July 1713) were favourable to Britain; they included the confirmation of

Britain's Gibraltar, and provided for the acquisition of Newfoundland in Canada and St Kitts (an important bargaining chip in Berkeley's ill-fated 'Bermuda project') in the West Indies. The great costs of the wars made the Crown utterly dependent on parliament for tax revenue and, starting in 1689, parliament was transferred from an occasional event into a permanent institution of government.

As the financial clout of the Crown diminished, so too did its political and cultural sway. While Anne kept up the ceremonial significance of the court, political and cultural activity successively moved towards the 'polite society' of wealthy nobility and the more socially inclusive London coffee houses (of which there were over 650 by 1714), and clubs. The public sphere was developing and the transmission of ideas through print was burgeoning with the lapse of the Licensing Act in 1695 and then further encouraged by the 'Statute of Anne' or 1710 Copyright Act, which introduced robust copyright regulation for authors (though not in Ireland, which made it something of a hotbed for cheap 'unofficial' editions of books and pamphlets) and also included provisions for the public interest, such as a legal deposit scheme. The early 1700s accordingly saw the birth of mass political culture.

In 1707 Scotland surrendered parliamentary independence in return for free trade, and the union of the United Kingdom of Great Britain came to be. In Ireland the idea of a union with England was met with mixed feelings. William Molyneux's influential *Case of Ireland's being Bound by Acts of Parliament in England, Stated* (1698) argued for independence. Ulster MP Henry Maxwell, in his *Essay towards a Union of Ireland with England* (1703) argued for a full union along Anglo-Scottish lines. England, however, was uncompromising in her stance on Ireland as a 'dependent and subordinate kingdom' and Ireland remained a colony.

BERKELEY'S LIFE AND WORKS

THE BEGINNING

Berkeley spent his childhood near Kilkenny, in the south of Ireland, and was at a young age destined for philosophy. As he puts in the delightful entry 266 in his personal *Notebooks* (1707–8) in the midst of developing his immaterialist philosophy: "Mem: that I was distrustful at 8 years old and Consequently by nature disposed for these new Doctrines." At 11 years of age he attended the prestigious secondary school Kilkenny College. It was a Protestant school that was closed during the reign of James II, and had only recently opened again after William's victory in Ireland. Jonathan Swift, the famous satirist and cleric, was a few years ahead of Berkeley at the school, and the two became close friends later in life.

In 1700 Berkeley entered Trinity College Dublin, which was founded by Queen Elizabeth in 1592 and was seen as the University of the Protestant Ascendancy in Ireland, with Catholics only being allowed to apply for admission in 1793. The years 1690 to 1750 saw extraordinary philosophical activity and achievement in Ireland. It centred on a group of thinkers connected to the university and to the autonomous Dublin Philosophical Society. One reason why Trinity College became a leading centre of philosophical development at this time is that, on William Molyneux's recommendation, it was the first university to engage with and fully realize the importance of the philosophical work that would come to define the first half of the 1700s, John Locke's *Essay concerning Human Understanding*. The new empiricist method Locke proposed was embraced on an institution-wide level, with the Provost St George Ashe (co-founder of the Dublin Philosophical Society with William Molyneux) taking a lively personal interest in the matter. As Molyneux reports to Locke in a letter from the 22 December 1692, he

> was the first that recommended and lent to the reverend provost of our university, Dr Ashe, a most learned and ingenious man, your essay, with which he was so wonderfully pleased and satisfied, that he ordered it to be read by the bachelors in the college, and strictly examines them in their progress.

In the *Essay* Locke examines the human mind in order to establish what our understanding is capable of knowing about the world we live in. His answer is that the building blocks for all our knowledge are 'ideas'. By 'idea' he means any identifiable part of mental phenomena, including both our experience of external things, and our awareness of inner events. His definition of idea in the *Essay* reads: "Whatsoever the mind perceives in itself, or in the immediate object of Perception, Thought or

Understanding" (2.8.8). He is seen as broadly adhering to an empiricist rather than rationalist position because he dedicates Part 1 of the *Essay* to arguing against the notion of 'innate ideas', maintaining instead that all ideas are acquired from experience. As there is no independent realm of truth accessible to the pure intellect it becomes central to Locke's approach that it is not philosophy itself but natural science that is the main source of human knowledge. He sees his role as philosopher as underlabourer (Locke, *Essay*, Epistle to the Reader), clearing up confusions and clarifying knowledge claims.

Most Irish philosophers at the time were broadly in agreement with the basic tenets of Locke's position, but a lively debate about the particulars quickly ensued. The first controversy concerned the nature of language, and more specifically the issue, as we would call it today, of 'cognitivism'. That is, whether language is meaningful only to the extent that it picks out specific conceivable items in the mind (namely Lockean ideas) of those who understand what is said, or whether it could be said to function properly if it bypasses such cognitive elements and, for example, directly raises emotions in the hearer. The second issue concerned perception, and in particular, it addressed the issue of how different sense modalities, such as sight, touch and hearing, are related. This was also couched in the Lockean terms of whether or not there are any ideas that are shared by several senses.

John Toland started the cognitivist debate with his *Christianity Not Mysterious* (1696). Like Locke, he employed a strict cognitivist semantics, holding that for something to be meaningful it must stand for a distinct idea. On this basis he reasoned that mysteries, such as the Holy Trinity might be thought to be, are something of which we have no clear idea. Therefore, either Christianity employs literally meaningless doctrines or it is free of mystery. This was immediately recognized as a dilemma that was a threat to established Christianity. If there are no mysteries, understood as something of which we have no clear idea, then much of Christian doctrine must be discarded. If, on the other hand, it is accepted that there are mysteries in Christianity, then we either have to accept that literal nonsense pervades these teachings, or we must reject the broadly Lockean cognitivist semantics. Toland's book was seen as a threat to established religion and met with violent opposition. It was burned by the common hangman in front of the

Irish parliament buildings in September 1697. Toland himself, not without reason, thought it prudent to leave the country.

Beside these uncivilized ways of shutting down Toland, a number of written responses also appeared. Peter Browne, fellow at and later Provost of Trinity College Dublin, replied in his *A Letter in Answer to a Book Entitled, Christianity Not Mysterious* (1697). His line of attack focused on the cognitivist element and is therefore an early example of critical engagement with Locke's philosophical project. Browne argued that it is too restrictive to say that every intelligible notion we have answers to a clear and distinct idea. Some things are known in a more roundabout way. Browne considers the attributes of God, such as omnipresence and infinity. Though we cannot form ideas of such things directly, we can make them intelligible by using other things to stand in for those. In the case of omnipresence, Brown suggested that we can make it understandable if we conceive of a continuously expanding space; in the case of infinity we can think of a continued addition of numbers. By manipulating our thoughts about things in our environment or our own mental operations, we are therefore able, Browne thinks, to form indirect ideas of religious mysteries by analogy.

From these specific issues of Church doctrine and semantics, Browne moves to the nature of perception. Here he considers a thought experiment in which he imagines the cognitive situation of a blind person. This person, he says, will hear others, who have sight, speak of light and colours. At first, this person might not believe what the others speak of. But she could be convinced that these things exist, not by acquiring distinct ideas of them, but by being convinced that others, who are at a distance from her, can perceive her actions when she, for example waves her hand. This experiment represents a concrete situation in which one would be justified in believing in something of which one does not, and indeed cannot, have an idea; thus, according to Browne, the strict cognitivism that Toland's argument depended on will crumble.

Around the same time William Molyneux was engaged in an extensive correspondence with Locke about a number of issues in his *Essay*. These discussions, later published as *Familiar Letters between Mr. Locke and Several of his Friends* (1708), occasioned several changes in the second (1694) edition of the *Essay*. Included in the second edition is a question posed by Molyneux in their correspondence, concerning the relation between perceptions from different sense modalities. The 'Molyneux problem' that Locke presented in *Essay* 2.9.8 is this: suppose that a man is born blind and able to distinguish different shapes, such as a cube and a sphere by touch. Further suppose that this man is suddenly made to see and that a cube and a sphere are placed in front of him. Would he, by sight alone, be able to tell which shape is which? Both Molyneux and Locke give a negative answer to this question. However, they differ in their motivation for this conclusion.

Molyneux simply states that we would have to learn to correlate what we see with what we touch by experience. For example, there is nothing in the corner of the square, as it appears visually, that, by itself, indicates that it is the same kind of thing as a corner as it appears to the tactile sensation, and so there are no direct visual cues that are similar to tactile experience, and which allow us to distinguish the visual square from the visual circle. Locke, on the other hand, held that there was indeed something shared between the visual and the tactile object, namely the idea of 'shape'. Locke assumes that what we receive through vision is a two dimensional representation of the object. Accordingly, he stated that what the blind man would see when he looked at the sphere for the first time would be a two dimensional image of a circle with various shades of colours. However, Locke argued, this visual information would not be enough for the blind man to determine that what he was looking at was indeed the sphere rather than the cube. He would have to walk around the objects and touch them to realize that the different shades of the two dimensional objects were indicators of three dimensional shape.

Locke's answer assumes a view of perception that goes back at least as far as Aristotle's *De Anima* (418ª). This is the doctrine of 'common sensibles', the view that different sense modalities such as vision and touch give us access to the same ideas, such as 'roundness' and 'square-ness'. If this claim about perception is true, then it naturally supports further doctrinal components that lie at the core of Locke's philosophical views. In particular, it would support his distinction between primary and secondary qualities. For Locke, a quality is the power of an object to produce ideas in us. Primary qualities, that is "Solidity, Extension, Figure, Motion or Rest, and Number" (*Essay* 2.8.9), belong to every particle of matter itself. As these qualities belong to the objects themselves, the ideas of sense corresponding to these are perceptions of the object as it is in itself. Secondary qualities are not really part of the outer objects. Rather, it is the power that primary qualities have by which they produce sensations in us, which they do by their bulk, figure and texture of the various particles of matter. These sensations, which are not in the objects themselves, are ideas like "Colours, Sounds and Tastes, etc" (*Essay* 2.8.10). So the ideas of secondary qualities do not answer to anything resembling them in the objects themselves. For example, that an object is perceived as blue is a consequence of the texture and figure of the object, its primary qualities, which causes it to reflect light in a certain way, that light then enters our eyes and results in an idea of blue. The sensation 'blue' is then nothing in the external world but only in the minds of perceivers.

This theory of qualities, leads naturally to the idea that primary qualities are 'common sensibles'. For since material things themselves have shape, size, and so on, it is not surprising that we can become aware of their shapes, sizes, and so on, more or less accurately, by way of more than one sensory channel. Further, if, for example, shapes as we see them and shapes as we feel them both resemble the shape that material things actually have, intrinsically, then these visible and tactile shapes will also resemble one another.

THE NEW THEORY OF VISION: OPENING THE GATES TO IMMATERIALISM

Berkeley's first major philosophical work was the *New Theory of Vision* (1709). One of his central aims in this book is to reject the theory of 'common sensibles'. Thus, a major part of his project in this work is to undermine an aspect of Locke's theory, which could eventually erode the central distinction between primary and secondary qualities, and ultimately the materialistic conception of the world upon which it depends. In this way Berkeley's *New Theory*, though narrow in scope when measured by philosophical standards, is the beginning of his attack on established philosophy as he understood it, and a first step towards his own immaterialist system.

Berkeley's aim in the *New Theory* is twofold. He wants to explain how spatial visual perception works and he wants to examine whether or not there are any shared sensibles. His conclusion about the first issue informs his views about the second issue. At the outset Berkeley makes a distinction between direct and indirect perception, which is crucial for his overall theory of perception. Direct perception refers to what we see, or feel, or taste, etc., at a particular moment without taking into account any judgement, anticipation, experience or heuristic of any kind. Another way of putting this is to say that direct perception is simply the perceptual data we receive from without, independently of any further processing done by our perceptual system. Indirect perception refers to our integrated experience of the world; it is full of background assumptions, prior experience, infused with cultural, historical, and scientific concepts and language. When Berkeley considers how spatial perception works, he is investigating whether we see spatial features, in particular 'distance', 'size' and 'situation' (roughly direction and position) directly or indirectly.

It is obvious that we see these features at least indirectly. It would be very strange to doubt that I can see that the screen I am now looking at is at a distance from me, that it has roughly the size that it has, and (most absurdly, to my mind at least) that the left side of the screen is to the left and the right side of the screen is to the right, and similarly with the directional polarities of up and down and in front and behind. Instead, what Berkeley is interested in is determining whether this information is included in the data we receive, or whether it is only a result of an, often significant, perceptual process. In the case of all three spatial features, Berkeley argues that we only see them indirectly. Further, he argues that we perceive these features directly by our sense of touch only. To see these features we must connect the visual data to the completely different tactile data through a perceptual process. If this account is true, then some of the prime candidates for being 'common sensibles', such as shape and size, are not, strictly speaking, shared between the sense of sight and touch, but are properly the objects of one sense, touch.

Berkeley first considers distance. It is, he says, agreed by all that "distance, of itself and immediately, cannot be seen" (*New Theory* §2). Berkeley appears right in this assertion, for it was explicitly stated by Molyneux in his authoritative *Dioptrica Nova* (1692: 113) and implied by Malebranche in his *Search* (1.9.1) that distance is a straight line from a starting point to an end point. If we saw distance directly, that would mean that we would see a line that has a starting point on our eye, and an end point on the object we are looking at.

But from our point of view, the lines, which would proceed straight from our eyes, would themselves appear to us like a point. If we saw distance directly all different distances would look the same, that is, they would look like a point.

Clearly, in our everyday experience we see all manner of things as being at all kinds of different distances. If distance is not given directly by the visual data, then our ability to see distance requires an explanation. Berkeley considers the typical kind of explanation, which he finds in the works of Descartes and Malebranche, and argues that their view is defective and that he has a better explanation. His opponents assume that there are two different ways in which we see distance. One account of how we determine distances is by empirical cues, such as whether the object looks faint or 'lively' and whether it looks large or small. Another explanation for the same phenomena is that we dispense with such cues and instead use a form of innate geometry, according to which the mind judges an object to be near or far depending on whether the angle between the two eyes and the object is acute, or obtuse. Berkeley thinks that there is a conflict in these two accounts that makes the view as a whole problematic.

With regard to things that are far away Berkeley takes it to be uncontroversial that we see the distance of an object by means of certain visible cues that we have experienced as going together with various distances (this explanation is also used by proponents of the geometrical theory). For example, we use other objects in our field of vision, which we have experienced as being at a certain distance and of a certain magnitude ("such as houses, fields, rivers, and the like", *New Theory* §3) to help us determine the distance of some other object (such as "yonder castle"). Another useful cue is the faintness or distinctness and the size of the object. If I have previously experienced the object to be distinct and large and now see it as smaller and less distinct I can with some confidence conclude that it is further away.

However, in cases in which an object is close to us the geometrical theory (Berkeley here refers to Descartes, *New Theory* §4) holds that we judge objects to be closer or further away (say, 10 or 20 centimetres from our eyes) by judging the largeness of the angle created by drawing lines from the centre of each eye to a point of the object. In this case we do not infer the distance of the object from experience but through geometrical reasoning.[1] In this way the geometrical theory can establish a necessary connection between the things we see and the distance (a larger angle necessarily means that the object is closer) which was not present in the case of seeing things far away, since the experiential cues such as size are not necessarily connected to larger or smaller distance, but other factors, such as distinctness, are also in place. For example, not all small things are far away, some things are actually small. The proponent of the geometrical theory is therefore seen by Berkeley to use different kinds of explanations of how we see. They use both inferences from experience when judging the distances of things far away and geometrical reasoning when judging the distances of things that are close to the eye. Berkeley's conclusion is that we always judge the distance of objects through experience and never by means of an innate geometry.

Berkeley's account of how we come to see the distances of things that are relatively close to us is that we do so by means of associations based on experiential cues that belong to the act of looking at the object. Berkeley gives two examples of such cues. Firstly, if I hold a pen half a metre in front of my eyes and move it slowly towards me while looking directly at the pen the pupils of my eyes will move closer together. The relative position of my pupils is accompanied by the unpleasant sensation of a strain to my eyes (try it yourself!) This degree of painful strain is therefore associated with changes in the distance of the object when it is relatively near to me. As Berkeley puts it,

I know [. . .] that the sensation arising from the turn of the eyes is of itself immediately perceived and various degrees thereof are connected with different distances, which never fail to accompany them into my mind, when I view an object distinctly with both eyes, whose distance is so small that in respect of the interval between the eyes has any considerable magnitude.

(*New Theory* §18)

Secondly, when moving the pen in the way described it will also look more and more confused or blurred and so from this visual blurriness and sharpness we also infer distance (*New Theory* §21).

The next spatial property that Berkeley examines is size. As with distance the size of an object is not immediately seen by vision neither according to the geometrical theory nor on Berkeley's view. The reason for this is quite straightforward. Some things can take up a large part of the visual field but still be small and a large thing can take up a small part of the visual field. By means of what, then, do we know if a thing that takes up a certain portion of the visual field is large or small? According to the geometrical theory we know this by combining the size of the object in my field of vision or on the retina with the distance of the object. For example, a person who is one metre tall, seen at 10 metres' distance, looks smaller than a three-metre-tall person at a distance of 20 metres because our visual system factors in the distance with the size of the immediate object of sight (*New Theory* §60).

Berkeley explains that the problem with this view is that since we know distance by means of certain experiential cues (as he claims to have established in his discussion on distance), and these cues are equally cues for size and distance, it is incorrect to claim that we first establish the distance of the thing and then its size. The associations that lead us to determining the distance of an object are the same associations that allow us to determine the size of it. The cues for distance are the visual cues of visual size, distinctness and faintness. If something takes up a large portion of our visual field and is blurry, then we take it to be small, and if something takes up a small portion of our visual field and is faint, then we take it to be large. In the first case we also expect the object to be close to us, for example a book that I hold up close to my eyes and in the second case we also take the object to be far away, for example a building that I see in the distance. So there is no priority of distance over size in these cues, they work equally for both.

Again, as with distance, the size we are referring to when we judge an object to have a certain magnitude is not the visual size but the tactile size. The visual size varies with the distance whereas the tactile size of an object remains the same and is the referent of visual size. "Whenever, therefore, we speak of the magnitude of anything, for instance a tree or a house, we must mean the tangible magnitude, otherwise there can be nothing steady and free from ambiguity spoken of" (*New Theory* §55). Therefore, according to Berkeley visible size is not necessarily connected to the actual, tactile magnitude of the object. This sets his view apart from the geometrical theory where there is a geometrical relation between the thing we see and the thing we touch.

Finally, Berkeley turns to situation. By situation he means the relations between the positions of objects, or parts of objects relative to each other, e.g., seeing a person's feet as being closer to the earth than the head when the person is standing up or seeing something as being to the left or right of something else. His discussion centres on the problem of the inverted retinal image. Berkeley presents the problem in the following way,

> There is at this day no one ignorant that the pictures of external objects are painted on the *retina*, or fund of the eye: that we can see nothing which is not so painted: and that, according as the picture is more distinct or confused, so also is the perception we have of the object: but then in this explication of vision there occurs one mighty difficulty. The objects are painted in an inverted order on the bottom of the eye: the upper part of any object being painted on the lower part of the eye: and so also as to right and left. Since therefore the pictures are thus inverted, it is demanded how it comes to pass that we see the objects erect and in their natural posture.
>
> (*New Theory* §88)

The problem is then that given that the light that reaches our eye will reflect on the retina in a way that is inverted compared to the situation of the light rays as they leave the object, why is it that we do not see the world as being upside down?

On the geometrical theory the answer is that based on the upside-down retinal image we trace back the rays of light from the angle they hit the retina to the object itself and so what we actually see is a picture that is the result of a geometrical calculation based on the retinal image (*New Theory* §89). Berkeley's objection to this view is, as always with the geometrical theory, that we are not conscious of any part of this geometrical reasoning process and that we do not see any light rays or the angles at which they enter the eye.

In fact, Berkeley's account of how we see situation and the *very problem* of seeing situation is different from the geometrical theory. Since he has already argued at length that we see only light and colour immediately and the situation of an object is not understood solely in terms of variations in these sensations it follows that situation cannot be an immediate object of sight. The immediate objects of sight are not at any determinate distance and do not have any determinate size, so it is impossible that their parts could be lower down or higher up than or left or right of each other. Rather, situation, like all spatial properties of objects, is, in the first instance, a tactile idea. So what Berkeley needs to explain is how we can see situation, given that situation is primarily tactile and not visual.

Again Berkeley's answer is that we learn through experience to correlate our tactile sensations with our visual. Berkeley's explanation for how we do this is that by moving our head or eyes we learn to correlate the visual changes with changes of direction and the location of our body and also by the force of gravity. It is by means of these latter cues that Berkeley thinks a blind person would arrive at the notion of situation (*New Theory* §93). Berkeley speaks specifically about the directional polarities of up and down since this is what is at issue with the problem of the inverted retinal image.

> By the motion of his [a blind person's] hand he might discern the situation of any tangible object placed within his reach. That part on which he felt himself supported, or towards which he perceived his body to gravitate, he would term lower, and the contrary to his upper; and accordingly denominate whatsoever object he touched.
>
> (*New Theory* §93)

Since Berkeley has already argued that visual sensation itself is not the sensation of something outside us without being correlated to tactile sensation it follows, he believes, that if the blind person were made to see, this person would have to learn how to connect his newly acquired visual sensation with situational cues. By moving his eyes or body downwards what he sees will change and this he will learn to understand as being visual sensation of something that is also further down. Therefore, situation is also seen through associating various cues. The cues by means of which this association is made are not visual sensations, however, as in the case with some distance and size cues (e.g., faintness and distinctness). Instead the cues are themselves tactile sensations such as the movement of the body in different directions or the movement of parts of the body, such as the hands and the eyes (*New Theory* §98).

Berkeley concludes that the immediate objects of vision and the immediate objects of touch are of different kinds or "heterogeneous" (*New Theory* §137) and that the only things to which spatial denominations apply are, strictly speaking, tactile. The properties Locke thought were projected from the objects to us through a number of sensory outlets are, according to Berkeley, only perceived by touch. There are, properly speaking, no shared sensibles. If Berkeley is correct then he has undermined a powerful reason for believing that a certain set of properties, namely size and shape, are more objective than certain other properties, such as colours and tastes.

Nevertheless, this might be a minor emendation in the greater scheme of things. According to the *New Theory*, the properties of shape, size, etc., are strictly speaking tactile properties that determine and fix our visual sensation and in this sense they are still more objective than strictly visual sensation. In one sense that is true, but in another sense Berkeley is deceiving his readers in the *New Theory*. As he explains in the *Principles* (§44), which he composes only a year later, not only did he assume that tangible properties are the settled referent of visual sensation, he also then assumed falsely, as he now reveals, that tangible objects exist in a mind-independent external world. In the *Principles* he explains that these objects do not have any independent existence, but are only so many sensations. Not only are there no common sensibles, there is no ontological difference between primary and secondary qualities. This reveals that Berkeley aims to strike at the heart of the early modern picture of a mind-independent external world populated with objects that possess mind-independent geometrical properties. Instead, according to Berkeley, the entire physical world, in all its aspects is completely mind-dependent. In this way, the argument against common sensibles developed in the *New Theory* for the foundation for a central component of Berkeley's immaterialism.

THE PRINCIPLES OF HUMAN KNOWLEDGE: THE CENTRAL ARGUMENT AND THE BOOK'S 'FAILURE'

In the *Principles* Berkeley uses the literary form of the 'treatise'. This is a sparse way of writing, which in contrast to an 'essay' or a 'dialogue', presents premises and conclusions without much context, or emphasis on correct methodology, and without much consideration of the full import of the arguments on the reader. In the lengthy Introduction to the work he attacks a conception of abstraction (that will be considered in Chapter 4) that he takes to be important for the belief in material substance. In the main part of the book Berkeley launches into a swift assault on material substance itself, and therefore on the modern philosophy associated with Descartes, Locke, and their followers.

In §3 he first states that it is obvious to all that our own thoughts and feelings only exist in our minds. But, he continues, it is also obvious that all sensible things exist only in a mind that perceives them. All we need is to consider what we mean by the term 'exist' when we talk about sensible things existing. When I say that the table in front of me exists, all I am saying is that I see it and feel it. When I leave the room and talk about the table existing, all I mean is that if I were in the room, then I could see it and touch it. It is, therefore, a truth about all sensible things that to be is to be perceived, as Berkeley puts it, their "*esse* is *percipi*" (§3). Yes, Berkeley concedes in §4, many people labour under the curious supposition that things like mountains, rivers and houses actually exist regardless of whether they are perceived or not. But given a moment's reflection on what we mean when we say that such things exist, they will surely accept that the "*esse*" of a mountain is "*percipi*". If we accept, as Berkeley thinks we should, given what he says in §3, that sensible things only exist in the mind, and we also realize that things like mountains and rivers are sensible things, it follows that they exist only in the mind. Continuing this brisk tempo, Berkeley begins §7 with the statement that: "From what has been said, it follows, there is not any other substance than *spirit*, or that which perceives." Accordingly, he purports to have reached his central conclusion, which is to overthrow both the Cartesian metaphysics and the Lockean theory of ideas, less than three pages in to his treatise.

Readers were not convinced. Berkeley's friend, Sir John Percival was lobbying for Berkeley in London, but his reports back to Berkeley were discouraging. Some prominent thinkers had read the book, in particular Samuel Clarke, a leading philosopher and defender of Isaac Newton, most famous for his correspondence with Leibniz, and William Whiston, the mathematician and theologian who succeeded

Newton as Lucasian Professor of Mathematics at the University of Cambridge. Percival had heard of their views about the *Principles* second-hand and reported on 30 October 1710 that:

> they think you a fair arguer, and a clear writer, but they say your first principles you lay down are false. They look on you as an extraordinary genius, and profess a value for you, but say they wished had employed your thoughts less on metaphysics, ranking you with Father Malebranche, Norris and another whose name I have forgot, all whom they think extraordinary men, but of a particular turn, and their labours of little use to mankind for their abstruseness.

> (*Works* 9: 11–12)

Significant here is that Clarke and Whiston thought Berkeley's "first principles" were false. They do not think Berkeley's problem is with his *conclusion* (though they certainly did not hold that to be true either), but rather that Berkeley has certain *premises* in his arguments that they take to be false. What premises are these? Berkeley's argument is most explicitly stated in §4, where he says: "For what are [sensible objects] but the things we perceive by sense? And what do we perceive besides our own ideas or sensations?" (*Principles* §4) The two premises are then (1) that sensible objects are perceived by means of the senses and (2) that ideas are the only things that are perceived by means of the senses. From this Berkeley infers that sensible objects are ideas. As ideas are just the immediate content of our consciousness, sensible objects are strictly speaking in the mind.

As a number of scholars such as Winkler (1989), Stoneham (2002), Dicker (2011) and Rickless (2013) have pointed out, this ignores the obvious and broadly Lockean rebuttal that even if we accept that what we immediately perceive are ideas, these ideas represent mind-independently existing physical objects that cause the ideas we have of them through their primary qualities. This reply points out that the term 'perceive' should be understood differently in (1) and (2). In (2) it is the case that we *immediately* perceive only our own ideas. However, since these ideas are not supposed to be identical with sensible things, in (1) it is correct to state that we *mediately* perceive sensible things. We perceive these sensible things, which are understood to be mind-independent physical objects, by virtue of the ideas *representing* these sensible things to us. The ideas represent these objects in a wholly non-mysterious way, namely, by being likenesses of the physical objects; for the ideas are caused by physical objects imprinting themselves on our senses. Berkeley's position at its core assumes the controversial claim that sensible qualities are nothing but ideas. In the *Three Dialogues* Berkeley sets out to argue for this claim.

AFTER THE *PRINCIPLES*

Berkeley was ordained a priest in the Anglican Church of Ireland in 1710. He published *Passive Obedience* in 1712, in which he defended a version of that Tory doctrine. For the contemporary reader, his short but rich account of the foundation of moral obligation at the beginning of the work is probably of greater interest. In 1713 he left Ireland for the first time to go to London to publish the *Three Dialogues*. Here he made the acquaintance of members of the literary elite. He became good friends with Joseph Addison, Richard Steele, and later with Alexander Pope and Jonathan Swift. The latter used his influence to help the young Berkeley (who was 18 years younger than Swift) in two important ways. He introduced Berkeley to the court where he met and befriended his namesake Lord Berkeley of Stratton (to whom the *Three Dialogues* is dedicated) and he also introduced Berkeley to Charles Mordaunt, Earl of Peterborough, who had recently been appointed Ambassador Extraordinary to Victor Amadeus, King of Sicily. On Swift's recommendation the Earl brought Berkeley with him to Italy in the capacity of chaplain.

The mission lasted from October 1713 to August 1714 and Berkeley travelled via Paris, Lyon, Turin and Genoa. The most significant event on the journey might have been his stay in Paris. He set up a meeting with the leading philosopher and Roman Catholic priest, Nicolas Malebranche, but it is not clear if they ever met. Berkeley returned to London about the time of the death of the Stuart Queen Anne and the accession to the throne of her closest Protestant relative, George I. Disgruntled Tories and Jacobites instigated the first 'Jacobite Rebellion' at this time and Berkeley, whose *Passive Obedience* had led to charges of Jacobitism against him, published anonymously the strongly anti-Jacobite *Advice to the Tories who have Taken the Oaths* (1715). At this time Berkeley also started to think about his career. He seems to have considered entering the employment of Lord Peterborough and was, at the same time, hoping for promotion in the Church.

However, nothing came of either idea. Instead Berkeley again went on another continental tour, one that was to last four years, from the autumn of 1716 to the autumn of 1720. He had accepted an offer of a tutorship from St George Ashe, the enthusiastic supporter of Locke's *Essay* and former provost of Trinity College Dublin, who was now the Bishop of Clogher. Due to poor health the Bishop's son George Ashe required a trustworthy companion for his continental tour. The idea was to travel through Italy and in the course of the four years the pair managed to visit most parts of the country, including the southern parts which was unusual at the time. Their movements during the first year are well documented thanks to Berkeley's extant travel diary that covers the period of January 1717 to April 1718. They explored Rome, Naples and later Sicily. Berkeley recorded observations and reports of the tarantula, the pathological disorders it caused, and the unorthodox method of relieving the symptoms, at the request of Dr Friend. He also climbed Mount Vesuvius and witnessed an eruption, the account of which was later published in *Philosophical Transactions* under the title "The eruption of Mount Vesuvius" (1717). While in Lyon, on the way back to London in 1720, Berkeley wrote *De Motu*, his main work on the philosophical foundations of natural science. He had in mind to submit it to the Royal Academy of Sciences at Paris as an entry to their essay competition on the nature of motion. Though Berkeley did not win the competition (indeed it is not clear whether his work was ever entered into the competition) he thought highly enough of it to have it published in London the following year.

In 1721 Berkeley returned to Ireland and relaunched his academic career. In November he was appointed Divinity Lecturer and Preacher in Trinity College Dublin. A year later he was appointed Senior Proctor and in June 1723 Hebrew Lecturer. In May 1724 Berkeley was made Dean of Derry, a position worth £700 per year. His financial position was now secure and he has the freedom to pursue his next great task – the Bermuda project. After coming back to

Britain from his Italian journey in the wake of the economic collapse known as the South Sea Bubble, Berkeley saw not only a country but a continent in moral and spiritual decline. He prophesized that the hope for western civilization lay in America. The plan was to build a college, named St Paul's, in Bermuda. English planters and native Indians would be invited (though, horrifically, the latter might also be kidnapped) to train there until they reached the level of MA at which point they could return to their own people as missionaries. Berkeley published his plan in *A Proposal for the Better Supplying of Churches in our Foreign Plantations and for Converting the Savage Americans to Christianity* (1724/5). The next two years found Berkeley relentlessly lobbying for the project. He raised about £5,000 through private subscriptions and worked towards acquiring a charter from the king to erect a college in Bermuda, which he received in June 1725. In May 1726 a majority of the House of Parliament voted for an address to the King for a public grant for the project worth about £20,000 which was to be obtained through the sale of land on the recently acquired Saint Kitts. However, there was no stated time limit within which this money was to be paid. It was in this period too that Berkeley wrote his most celebrated poem, "Verses on the prospect of planting arts and learning in America" (published in the *Miscellany*, 1752), which includes the celebrated last stanza:

Westward the course of empire takes its way;
The first four acts already past,
A fifth shall close the drama with the day;
Time's noblest offspring is the last.

In 1728 Berkeley made his own way westward to supervise the Bermuda project and signal the seriousness of his intent to the UK parliament. Earlier the same year, he had married Anne Forster, daughter of John Forster, Recorder of Dublin, the Irish Chief Justice and Speaker of the Irish House of Commons. Anne had a serious intellectual disposition and was a religious mystic and follower of the leaders of the Quietist sect, Madame Guyon and François Fénelon. In September 1728 George and Anne Berkeley set sail for the New World and arrived in Newport, Rhode Island, in January the following year. The Berkeleys settled there

'stuff' that belongs uniquely to the object. The form, which is either substantial or accidental, is what gives the object its essential and inessential properties and qualities. Change in an object and causal interaction are, according to this account, explained in terms of the loss or acquisition of one or more of its forms and/or qualities. Any causal explanation of an event is, therefore, a matter of assigning the correct forms and qualities to the substances involved.

These sorts of explanations were deemed to be problematic because they were thought to engage more in a descriptive project than an explanatory one. The textbooks produced in 'the Schools' were concerned with categorizing natural phenomena and dividing them into genera and species rather than explaining how the phenomenon in question is produced. For example, Descartes lamented that the phenomenon of gravity was explained by the property of 'heaviness' of bodies and Boyle similarly complained that the whiteness of a body was explained in terms of the presence of 'white' in it (Descartes *Principles* Preface, AT VIII, CMS 182–3; Boyle *Origin of Forms and Qualities*, Boyle 1979: 16). Thus, the principles required for explaining phenomena are too many, for often the *explanans* (the explanation) and the *explanandum* (the thing in need of explanation) are the same and so the principles multiply with the phenomena.

The approach taken by the new, modern natural philosophers was to develop physics into a rigorously mathematical and mechanical discipline. Kepler (1551–1630), Galileo (1564–1642), Descartes (1596–1650), Boyle (1627–91), Newton (1642–1727), and others, made great strides in the mathematization and mechanization of nature that is the hallmark of the modern understanding of the world. This project sought to unite two ideas, which would allow natural science to be understood mathematically: *first*, the view that events in nature are similar to the motion of a vast machine, such as a complex clock; *second*, the idea that the essential workings of any mechanical system (such as a clock or the physical world) can be captured by an abstract mathematical model. Together with the project of explaining natural phenomena mathematically there was also a concerted effort to develop various conceptions of material nature that would support the mechanistic vision of physical reality, such as those developed by Descartes, Gassendi (1592–1655), Hobbes (1588–1679), Locke, and others.

DESCARTES

It is in Descartes' philosophical underpinning for this conception of nature that we can see the idealist current, which came to permeate modern thought. Indeed, both Hobbes and Gassendi (in the third and fifth set of replies to the *Meditations*, respectively) put forward materialist criticisms of Cartesian dualism.[2] According to Descartes metaphysical system there is one uncreated and wholly independent substance – God (*Principles* 1.51). There are two other substances that are dependent for their existence only on God: mind, defined in terms of the activity of thinking, and matter, defined as extension in three dimensions (*Principles* 1.52). This division raises a number of questions about the possibility of causation. Returning to the provisional definition of idealism above, one might hold, as some philosophers evidently have, that for something to be real it must, in some sense, be capable of acting.[3] On this view we are guided by what is active in the world. A causal theory, which states that mind is the only active thing, could therefore be understood as an immaterialist position.

One general problem for the Cartesian conception of two really distinct substances is that it is not clear how radically different kinds of things can causally affect each other. Another problem pertains specifically to the causal efficacy of matter. Mind has, as it were, activity built in to its definition. Thinking, imagining, and remembering, are all in some sense the generation of thoughts or ideas. Though Descartes does not accept that there is a mode of action that is shared between our minds and God, he does accept that the only model appropriate to representing the way in which God moves bodies, is the way in which we are aware of moving our own bodies through thought (AT V, 347, CSMK 375). Matter, on the other hand, is defined by its inert geometrical property of extension. While such a definition makes it fully accessible to mathematics, it is not clear how there can be genuine activity in a system comprised entirely of matter. Nevertheless, bodies move, undergo change in shape, size and motion, and collide with other bodies. What, then, is the cause of these changes on Descartes view?

One approach, explored by Garber (1993) is to deny any genuine causal activity to bodies and to explain all bodily interaction in terms of God's activity, and so to take Descartes to be an 'occasionalist' with regard to body–body causation. It is clear that according to Descartes God creates and maintains all things in existence. He further holds that in 'creating' and in 'sustaining in existence' the same force and action is exercised (*Meditations* III, AT VII, 49; *Principles* 2.36). It appears, then, that God is the cause of all motion in accordance with the laws of nature that he has ordained. A different view defended by Della Rocca (1999) and Pessin (2003) is to hold that Descartes held a 'concurrentist' position according to which both God and bodies are responsible for changes in bodies. Descartes perhaps comes closest to stating something like this in *Principles* 2.40. However, as Schmaltz (2005) has pointed out, it is far from clear that such a view is consistent with Descartes' 'thin', merely geometrical, conception of material substance or that it does not lead to causal over-determination, that is, that there are more causes than is necessary to explain the phenomena.

Similar issues arise in the case of body–mind causation. From what has been stated above it seems doubtful that matter could fulfil the role of a causal agent. Conceptually it is not clear how the mode of extension can involve the notion of force or power. Further, Descartes' view of body–body causation suggests that God is the only active force involved in the movement of bodies. However, in the sixth meditation proof for the existence of material substance (to be considered in more detail below) he states that corporeal things have the "active faculty" that corresponds to the "passive faculty" of sensation and so he appears to state that matter is the cause of perceptions in us. But, as Garber (1993: 20–1) has pointed out, in the corresponding passage in the *Principles* (2.1), written three years later, there is no mention of a causal relation between objects and our ideas of them. The French edition, published three years after the Latin original, suggestively states that corporeal things *occasion* the ideas we have of them. On the available evidence it is not clear whether Descartes took corporeal things to have any genuine causal power or whether he held, also with regard to purported body–mind causation, that God is the true cause of sensations on the occasion of certain motions (themselves created and sustained by God) of bodies. This discrepancy between the features of Descartes' two created substances led later thinkers, such as Leibniz and of course Berkeley, to seriously entertain the idea that only a mind or something mind-like could in fact be a substance.

As a result of these apparent ambiguities, those who broadly followed Descartes' programme aimed to locate causation solely in either immaterial or material substance. One direction taken by 'Cartesianism' was, accordingly, towards the immaterial 'occasionalist' view. For example, Malebranche took Descartes to have ruled out divine concurrentism with the doctrine of 'continuous creation' (Malebranche *Search*, Elucidation 15, OMC 3:238). Another path was paved by Regis who developed a conception of bodies acting as 'secondary causes', but in doing so he explicitly distances himself from Descartes' account of 'continuous creation' (Regis *Use of Reason and Faith* 1704, 322).

Another way of examining the nature of reality could be to search for something of which we are indubitably certain, and take this perfect and unquestionable kernel of truth as a model for what is real. An epistemic theory that states that the most certain thing is the awareness of oneself as a thinking being would, by this method, lead to the possibility of immaterialism. In the *Meditations* Descartes employs the sceptical method in order to discover what he can know with certainty. In the second meditation he discovers that he can be certain of the existence of one thing, his own existence (as long as he thinks) (AT VII, 25). He is also certain that the thoughts and experiences he has, qua contents of his mind (but not as outer objects or signs of outer objects), exist (AT VII, 29). He does not find himself in the same position with regard to matter. To have knowledge about a body, such as a piece of wax, we require a judgement on the basis of a perception (AT VII, 32). We are therefore required to make an inference about an outer object on the basis of a mental item within my mind, and such an operation is always prone to the possibility of error. In this way we are always more 'certain', that is, our knowledge is of a higher degree of probability, about the contents of our mind than external things. The existence of the mind is also more evident, there are more confirming instances. Any purported case of sense experience, and in addition all inner perception, gives us evidence of the existence of a mental substance (*Principles* 1.11; *Meditations* II, AT VII, 33, CSM 22). Therefore "every consideration whatsoever which contributes to my perception of the wax, or of any other body, cannot but establish even more effectively the nature of my own mind" (*Meditations* II, AT VII, 33, CSM 22).

To remedy this epistemic disparity between the two created substances, Descartes presents a proof for the existence of material objects in the sixth meditation already alluded to above. It begins by noting that we passively receive sensations and that these sensations must originate in something distinct from my mind (*Meditations* VI, AT VII, 79, CSM 55). This thing is either a mind (like God or some other "creature more noble than a body", or matter. Descartes rules out the first alternative because we have no resource for discovering such a source for our sensation. On the other hand, he maintains, we have been given a "great propensity to believe" that the sensations are produced by a corporeal nature (*Meditations* VI, AT VII, 80, CSM 55). It follows that God would be a deceiver if sensations were not transmitted from material things. Since God is not a deceiver, it follows that corporeal things exist.

This argument would come under intense scrutiny by later thinkers. One set of worries is that Descartes' arguments in *Meditations* 3–6 are shaky at best, depending as they do on the ontological argument for God's existence and on the veracity of 'clear and distinct ideas'. Perhaps, then, Descartes is stuck at the sceptical position of the second meditation with the existence of material substance, at best, only a possibility. However, even if the existence of a non-deceiving God and the legitimacy of 'clear and distinct ideas' are granted, the claim that we have a God-given belief (rational or otherwise) in material substance was also challenged, putting, as we shall now see, further pressure on the tenability of the existence of material substance.

MALEBRANCHE

Though Malebranche was not himself strictly an immaterialist, he took decisive steps toward addressing the outstanding problems mentioned above in ways that made the immaterialist alternative to Cartesian dualism all the more palatable. His causal theory states that God is the only genuine cause of any event in the world and so explicitly for-mulates a global occasionalist position. Malebranche has a number of arguments for his view. The two most relevant in the present context are, first, the so-called 'no necessary connections' argument and the 'conservation is but continuous conservation' argument. The former states that a true cause requires a necessary connection between the cause and effect. However, within the world, it is always conceiv-able that something intervenes with one event leading to another. Malebranche particularly emphasizes the possibility that God could always intervene to thwart any worldly event following from another (*Search* 450). Instead, the only necessary connection that exists is between God's will and its effects (*Search* 450). Does this argument lead to the conclusion that God is the only cause? Many thinkers at the time would have thought that there was still room for a 'concurrentist' position. Just because God could interfere with events does not mean that he initiates every event. At most, we could say that for a non-divine cause to lead to an event, God's assent is required. Instead, as suggested above, Malebranche's most powerful argument might invoke the idea of causation as continuous creation.

With regard to the epistemic problem, Malebranche thinks that any argument based on sense perception will be susceptible to the systematic misrepresentations of sense (*Search* 573). Neither does he accept Descartes' proof for the existence of corporeal things in the sixth meditation. Assuming that Descartes has demonstrated the existence of a non-deceiving God, it is not sufficient to point to an alleged propensity to believe in matter. Instead, Malebranche requires a demonstration that God "has assured us that He has really created such a world, which proof I have not found in the works of Descartes" (*Search* 573). As neither sense nor reason are sufficient to make us certain that bodies exist there is only one option left, faith in the Bible's account of creation (*Search* 574).

Malebranche's own positive account of knowledge of external bodies and mathematical truths is summarized in his remarkable claim that "we see all things in God" (*Search* 230). Though much of Malebranche's conception of seeing all things in God is explicitly modelled on Augustine's doctrine of divine illumination, Malebranche claims that Augustine could not develop that position into a comprehensive account of knowledge. The reason for this was that Augustine could not have been aware of recent scientific developments in perception, in particular regarding the nature of vision (OC 6:68). Augustine, according to Malebranche, thought that colours are in physical objects. As colours are changeable, he could not say that the colours, and therefore objects, are perceived in God. Therefore, as we see objects entirely by colours, our subjective and changeable experience of objects just is what objects are. The objects we see in God, the archetypical structure that is equivalent to ultimate reality, must be immutable and the same for everyone, therefore Augustine could not say that we see objects in God. The correct view, which Malebranche suggests was first presented by Descartes, instead holds that sensible qualities are mere modifications of the mind, purely subjective experience, whereas objects, that is, material things, are non-sensible objects with purely geometrical properties (*Search* xxvi). It is only by accepting the distinction between aspects of objects that are modifications of our own mind, subjective aspects, and the unchangeable, objective and geometrical aspects, that we can maintain the identification of knowledge of the world with the knowledge of a perfect and unchangeable divinity. On Malebranche's account, God causes (as he causes everything, given global occasionalism) the ideas and sensations in our mind. When I perceive the sun, God causes me to sense yellow and to have the idea of roundness. The changeable sensation of colour is not, however, something we see in God but something that exists only in our mind. The roundness, however, is a stable geometrical property that is (probably) in the sun itself, and so this idea is not only caused by God but 'in God' as creator of the sun.

Two aspects of Malebranche's theory of knowledge are worthy of emphasis here. First, he does not accept Descartes' argument for the existence of bodies in the sixth meditation. Instead of attempting to provide a different argument, Malebranche transfers the belief in the existence of bodies from the realm of science and philosophy to the realm of religious authority. By making the conviction of the existence of outer objects a matter of faith rather than of knowledge, he was perceived by many other thinkers to give in to a form of scepticism about outer objects. Second, by stating that sensible qualities are nothing more than modification of our souls, and by, at the same time, maintaining that material objects have purely intellectual spatial properties, Malebranche again seems to widen the chasm between the kind of information available to human beings and the nature of reality. In this way, his emphasis on the reality and efficacy of mental substances was paired with an epistemological view that smacked of scepticism. Malebranche, therefore, already burdened immaterialist metaphysics with scepticism about the outer world, even before Berkeley had the opportunity to formulate his strictly immaterialist position. This Malebranchian baggage informs much of Berkeley's strategy for presenting his position, but also prejudiced readers of Berkeley's work from the outset.

BERKELEY

How does Berkeley situate himself within this debate? In terms of the Cartesian metaphysical framework, Berkeley only admits of one kind of substance, mind or spirit (*Principles* §7). With regard to Descartes' sixth meditation argument, Berkeley rejects the idea that the propensity to believe in matter is given by God. Instead he argues that taking confused human thought and language for literal truth has led to the belief in incoherent 'general abstract ideas' involved in believing that the qualities and modes of matter can exist out of a mind (*Principles* Introduction §§21–4, Part I §§5, 11, 54–6; *Three Dialogues* 3:243). Showing the prevalence of this kind of mistake is only a part of Berkeley's attack on the notion of material substance. He proceeds by arguing that all sensible qualities, including all primary qualities, are mind-dependent and that the concept of material substance, which includes both the sensible quality of extension and the idea of mind-independence, is self-contradictory (*Principles* Part I §§17, 24). Physical objects are sensible ideas or collections thereof (*Principles* Part I §§1, 3, 148; *Three Dialogues* 1:195, 3:249).

This conception of physical objects directly influences Berkeley's view on causation. According to Berkeley's immaterialist view bodies, being nothing but sensible ideas, are inert (*Principles* §25). Mind, soul or spirit can be known, through introspection, to cause ideas by an act of will (*Principles* I §28). Since the ideas of physical objects are not created by my act of will, there must be another spirit, namely God, who wills them (*Principles* §§29–33). Therefore, with regard to causation bodies cannot be the cause of anything (*De Motu*, §§22–4, 26–9, 31) and so Berkeley agrees with "Cartesian philosophers" who "recognize God as the principle of natural motions" (*De Motu* §32). Body–body causation and body–mind causation are therefore changes that are to be explained in terms of God's actions. On the issue of whether finite minds can cause changes in bodies (i.e., create new sensible ideas in one's own mind or in that of others), things are not so clear. Sometimes Berkeley states that we can directly influence the sensible ideas associated with our own body. In his early private *Notebooks* he famously proclaimed: "We move our Legs our selves: 'tis we that will their movement. Herein I differ from Malebranche" (§548). In the

Principles Berkeley only affirms that finite minds can create ideas of imagination (*Principles* §28) and seems to suggest that all sensible ideas are caused by God (*Principles* §§29–30). In *De Motu* he is explicitly ambivalent between the two views: "our mind at will can stir and stay the movements of our limbs, whatever be the ultimate explanation of the fact. [. . .] bodies are moved at the will of the mind, and accordingly the mind can be called, correctly enough, a principle of motion, a particular and subordinate principle indeed, and one which itself depends on the first and universal principle" (*De Motu* §25). Here Berkeley either suggests the concurrentist view or some form of occasionalism. In a later passage of the *Principles* Berkeley seems to suggest that we are responsible for the change of ideas of our body but that God is responsible for making those ideas present to others (and presumably also to ourselves) (*Principles* §147).

The idea of the interaction between corporeal things was on the early modern conception closely connected with the overall large-scale model of nature as a clock-like machine. On the deepest level, Berkeley's philosophical position aims to replace the cosmological model of the world as a machine with a language-based model. His constructive project is to analyse the structure of the connection between different kinds of sensible ideas in terms of a semiotic relation. In Berkeley's words "the connexion of ideas does not imply the relation of *cause* and *effect*, but only of a mark or *sign* with the thing *signified*" (*Principles* §65). On this view the world is not a giant clock but a book, or perhaps better, a conversation (*New Theory* §152). This, he argues, shows that nature is literally the language of God (*Alciphron* IV). Berkeley's endpoint is, in one sense, a unique philosophical position, which takes an empiricist theory of perception, a minimalist, often nominalist account of metaphysics, and ends up with the sort of broadly Neoplatonist theological vision that we find in Malebranche. His criticism of matter is only the starting point for this much more ambitious project.

INTRODUCING HYLAS AND PHILONOUS

In the *Three Dialogues* Berkeley opted for a daring stylistic approach. A philosophical dialogue is a quite specific kind of text in which the characters involved become important to the very meaning of the text. The scene in which the dialogue is set has a context or setting and the characters have deeply entrenched presuppositions or core beliefs. The characters possess varying levels of argumentative skill and, correspondingly, argumentative or intellectual shortcomings. They will use a certain amount of rhetoric and try to tailor their arguments to convince not the general public, but just the person with whom they are arguing. In a dialogue it is therefore useful to keep these attributes of the characters, in this case, Hylas and Philonous, in mind.

Hylas comes from the Greek word for 'matter' (ὕλη) and Philonous, in Greek, means 'lover of mind'. Thus, within the context of the dialogue, Hylas is someone who believes in the existence of material substance. Philonous, on the other hand, is an immaterialist who does not think there are any things other than minds and ideas in the world. Does that mean that Philonous is merely a mouthpiece for Berkeley? The answer, I think, is no, because Philonous says a number of things that are in opposition to each other. In the first dialogue he tacitly assumes certain premises that Berkeley would never have accepted. Sometimes he assumes some central aspect of the materialist doctrine to show how it conflicts with another core belief, and sometimes he states materialist claims so that his view will not seem too strange to Hylas, in an effort to, as it were, ease or lull Hylas into the clutches of immaterialism. We must, therefore, be careful, especially in the first dialogue, and not say "Berkeley says this", when presenting Philonous' position; we must, that is, keep the context in which Philonous' arguments are framed in mind. As David Berman (2005) has shown, this general caution is particularly warranted when we are dealing with Berkeley as he took *ad hoc* arguments and mild dissembling to be important weapons in his rhetorical arsenal. For example, in an autobiographical remark he confesses "He that would win another over to his opinion must seem to harmonize with him at first and humour him in his way of talking. From my childhood I had an unaccountable turn of thought that way" (*Works* 9:153).

What more do we know about these characters? As Tom Stoneham (2002) has explained, they are members of the same university. The book was written while Berkeley was a fellow at Trinity College Dublin, so it is reasonable to assume that they both belong to that institution. Hylas has a lower position than Philonous in the university. We know this by the way they talk to each other. For example, when Philonous says "I'll meet you here tomorrow to continue our discussion", or uses the imperative "we will". On the other hand, when Hylas arranges the meeting for the third day, he does not use the imperative but rather says that he would be glad if they could meet up the next day. Hylas is probably something like a postgraduate and Philonous is a professor or a fellow (as Berkeley was at the time).

Why did Berkeley choose to write a dialogue? A dialogue is like a literary or psychological description of a belief. When Hylas is shown to be wrong on some point he does not automatically accept Philonous' alternative, whereas in a more straightforward philosophical work, such as the *Principles*, you argue for something, assume it to have been proven and accepted, and move on to the next step in the argument. Instead, here we see Hylas finding himself at a loss or retracing his steps. He often does not quite know what to think, and he often needs to take a break, sometimes for a few minutes, sometimes overnight, to figure out replies and to take in what has been said. In this way the dialogue is a description of a belief, or rather, of two opposed beliefs. And we, the readers, can stand back and see how the characters react to each other's arguments. We are not directly told what to believe and so a dialogue is less imposing and less offensive. Through this more relaxed approach Berkeley wants to show why he thinks his brand of philosophy, immaterialism, is so compelling, whereas in the *Principles* we find a relentless attack on the reader's presuppositions.

Another obvious reason why one would use the dialogue form is that it allows you to put the opinions of those with whom you disagree in the mouth of a fictional character, in this case Hylas, without attacking them explicitly. In this way Hylas becomes a stand-in for a wide array of mostly early modern philosophers such as Hobbes, Locke, Descartes and Malebranche, but as we will see in Chapter 6, possibly also some medieval and ancient philosophers as well. With this change of tactic, Berkeley hoped to have more success in presenting his philosophy. In one way it was a success, it was more widely read than the *Principles* and translated into numerous languages. But, it did, in fact, have little impact in winning people over to his views.

NOTES

1 As Stoneham (2017) has pointed out, Berkeley's understanding of scepticism probably also drew on Diogenes Laertius' entry on 'Pyrrho' in his *Lives of Eminent Philosophers*.

2   See Garber (2012) for a recent discussion of this episode.
3   "A *Substance* is a being capable of action", Leibniz *Principles of Nature and Grace* (AG 207). "[A]ctivity is of the essence of a substance in general", Leibniz *New Essays* 65.

FURTHER READING

For a general overview of scepticism in early modern thought see Richard Popkin, *The History of Scepticism*. It exists in many editions; the most recent offering is *The History of Scepticism: From Savonarola to Bayle* (Oxford University Press 2003). Berkeley's relation to scepticism is discussed by Popkin in his essay "Berkeley and Pyrrhonism" in *The High Road to Pyrrhonism* (Hackett 1980) and in Tom Stoneham, "Berkeley's three dialogues between Hylas, Philonous and the sceptic" in Richard Brook and Bertil Belfrage (eds), *The Bloomsbury Companion to Berkeley* (Bloomsbury 2017).

There are a number of helpful anthologies on the development of modern philosophy up to and including Berkeley. Daniel Garber and Michael Ayers (eds), *The Cambridge History of Seventeenth-Century Philosophy* (1998) and Aaron Garrett (ed.), *The Routledge Companion to Eighteenth Century Philosophy* (2014). The classic expression of Berkeley's language model as an alternative to the mechanization and mathematization project of modern philosophy is Colin Turbayne, *The Myth of Metaphor* (University of South Carolina Press 1962). Kenneth Pearce, *Language and the Structure of Berkeley's World* (Oxford University Press 2017) offers a recent account of the role of language in Berkeley's overall project.

In-depth accounts of the setting of the *Three Dialogues* are found in Tom Stoneham, *Berkeley's World* (Oxford University Press 2002), chapter 2, and Aaron Garrett, *Berkeley's Three Dialogues: A Reader's Guide* (Continuum 2008), chapter 3.

3

THE NATURE OF THE SENSIBLE I

'Tis prudent to correct mens mistakes without altering their
language. This makes truth glide into their souls insensibly.

Notebooks §185

The first dialogue is in large part an argument for the assumption implicit
in the argument for immaterialism in the *Principles*, that sensible things
are nothing but ideas. One important part of the argument is to both
specify what the *process* of perception and the *object* of perception is.
The other central part of the argument requires Berkeley to move from a
notion of perception and sensation to the conclusion that sensible things
are nothing but ideas. This project requires Berkeley to make explicit
many of his theoretical claims and assumptions about how perception
works and what sensible things are, which were expressed in the *New
Theory* and the *Principles*. When moving from the characterization of
what is sensible (colours? mountains? other minds?) to *what the sensible
is* (atoms? ideas?), he both marshals the classical sceptical arguments
refined by Bayle, and draws extensively on his own deep considerations
of the issue from the *Notebooks* and elsewhere.

A CHALLENGE

The story begins with Philonous finding Hylas pacing around in a garden. Hylas is considering the "odd fate" (171) of those people who spend their lives in pursuit of knowledge only to profess ignorance about all things, that is to say, the sceptics. It transpires that Philonous also thinks that this tendency towards doubt is suspect, and claims instead to have taken up the vulgar, unphilosophical opinions of the common man. Hylas then says that the previous night he had taken part in a conversation about Philonous' philosophical views. In this discussion it was said that he denies the existence of material substance. To deny matter, "the very stuff of the world", seems to Hylas to be the most extravagant departure from the common sense of mankind, such that if Philonous is ready to deny this, he cannot conceivably believe in anything with conviction. Therefore, as Philonous now claims to be of the common opinion and not a sceptic, he thinks that Philonous must have given up on that dangerous philosophical outlook. Philonous replies that he has not given up on his position but that there is nothing repugnant to common sense in denying the existence of material substance and that it does not lead to scepticism. Hylas finds this very strange, and, at this point, they begin their discussion.

The first thing they do is agree on what a sceptic is. That is someone who either doubts or suspends judgement about all things, or someone who denies the reality and truth of things. The word 'things' can either stand for "universal intellectual notions", the principles and theorems of science, or 'things' can stand for sensible things. The sense of scepticism they are interested in turns out to be the scepticism that denies or suspends judgement about the second kind of things, sensible things. Having defined scepticism and the range of things that their sense of scepticism is about, we are then presented with the crux of what the *Three Dialogues* is going to be about. It is going to be a competition in which the winner is he who turns out to be the least sceptical in his philosophical account of sensible things.

DIRECT AND INDIRECT PERCEPTION

In order to begin their competition, they need to agree on some central terms by which they will be able to compare their respective views. The first such term is 'sensible thing'. After some prodding by Philonous, Hylas agrees with him that a sensible thing is something that is perceived immediately by sense. What does it mean to perceive something *immediately* by sense, as opposed to *mediately*? Philonous gives a number of examples of the contrast between mediate and immediate perception.

First they consider the contrast between immediate sensation and what is mediate in the sense of being *suggested* by it. The example they look at is the case of letters forming words that are written in a book and the notions that these words signify:

P: What mean you by sensible things?

H: Those things which are perceived by the senses. Can you imagine that I mean anything else? [. . .]

P: Suffer me then to ask you this farther question. Are those things only perceived by the senses which are perceived immediately? Or may those things properly be said to be *sensible*, which are perceived mediately, or not without the intervention of others?

H: I do not sufficiently understand you.

P: In reading a book, what I immediately perceive are the letters, but mediately, or by means of these, are suggested to my mind the notions of God, virtue, truth, etc. Now, that the letters are truly sensible things or perceived by sense, there is no doubt: but I would know whether you take the things suggested by them to be so too.

H: No certainly, it were absurd to think God or Virtue sensible things, though they may be signified and suggested to the mind by sensible marks, with which they have an arbitrary connexion.

P: It seems then, that by sensible things you mean those only which can be perceived immediately by sense.

H: Right. (174)

While the letters are immediately perceived, what they signify is not immediately perceived, but requires a process of language learning to allow us to move from sign to signified. We might think that Berkeley did not choose very good examples to explain this difference. After all, things like 'God' and 'virtue' are not themselves sensible things in the first place, therefore, the reason why Hylas agrees that we do not perceive them by sense is perhaps that they are things that cannot be perceived by sense under any circumstance, neither immediately nor mediately.

Let us therefore consider the case of the words of sensible things such as 'green' and 'chair'. Do I immediately or mediately perceive greenness when I read the word 'green' and the chair when I read the word 'chair'? On the one hand, it seems that the ideas of green and of a chair spring up in our mind at the very moment we read the words. This directness is even more evident if we consider the spoken words. It is almost impossible to disentangle the meaning of a word that we hear from the sounds associated with that meaning in a language we understand. You can easily test this by trying to hear only the sound of the words spoken by someone speaking in a language you understand, and ignore what they signify. Nevertheless, if we follow Hylas and Philonous' reasoning we must conclude that we perceive the greenness and the chair mediately. If we see words in a language we do not understand, or if we see a word we do not know the meaning of, there is no accompanying idea suggested. The process of learning which ideas to connect with various words requires that we first learn what the words stand for and that we understand the broader context of what is being expressed. What the directness of the association between word and meaning suggests is, therefore, that the connection is very powerful and effortless, once it is learned. In the *New Theory* Berkeley had argued that the relation between immediate objects of sensation (colours, tactile experience) and mediate objects (physical objects, the three dimensional expanse of experience) are similarly strongly but contingently connected.

The other example Hylas and Philonous discuss is the cause of immediate sensation:

> P: Doth it not follow from this, that though I see one part of the sky red, and another blue, and that my reason doth thence evidently conclude there must be some cause of that diversity of colours, yet that cause cannot be said to be a sensible thing, or perceived by the sense of seeing?
>
> H: It doth.
>
> P: In like manner, though I hear variety of sounds, yet I cannot be said to hear the causes of those sounds.

H: You cannot.

P: And when by my touch I perceive a thing to be hot and heavy, I cannot say with any truth or propriety, that I feel the cause of its heat or weight.

H: To prevent any more questions of this kind, I tell you once for all, that by *sensible things* I mean those only which are perceived by sense, and that in truth the senses perceive nothing which they do not perceive immediately: for they make no inferences. The deducing therefore of causes or occasion from effects and appearances, which alone are perceived by sense, entirely relates to reason.

P: This point then is agreed between us, that *sensible things are those only which are immediately perceived by sense.* (174–5)

Here Philonous trades on a distinction between the two different mental faculties of sensation and of reason, which was common in Berkeley's time. Sensation is a receptive faculty that receives data from the interaction between the outside world and our sense organs. Reason is the faculty used to logically organize information received from the senses and from internal awareness of oneself in order to form beliefs and make decisions. This reasoning activity involves inferring and deducing causes for those things that we immediately perceive. For example, if a stone is heated by the sun, by feeling the warmth when I hold the rock, I do not directly sense the cause of that warmth, namely the heat of the sun. If I am standing in a desert and touch the warm rock I can be quite certain that the heat is caused by the sun, but it still requires me to make the (very easy) inference about what caused the heat. If a stone heated by the sun were brought in to a house that had a roaring fire and a radiator on, there would be a number of candidate causes for the warmth in the rock and the correct inference would be more difficult to make.

If we accept with Hylas and Philonous that we do not immediately perceive by sense the *causes* of that which we immediately perceive, and that we do not immediately perceive by sense that which is *suggested* by what we immediately perceive, then what is left? Hylas and Philonous quickly agree that what is left are sensible qualities. That is to say, light, colours, sounds, tastes, odours and tangible qualities. In Philonous' words: "Sensible things therefore are nothing else but so many sensible qualities, or combinations of sensible qualities" (175).

In this opening discussion of the nature of the sensible Hylas and Philonous have accordingly reached two important conclusions. First, that a sensible thing is nothing but what is immediately perceived by sense. Second, that what is immediately perceived by sense is sensible qualities. With these points agreed upon, the next task for Philonous is to argue the points, assumed in the *Principles*, that sensible qualities are nothing but ideas, that is to say, mind-dependent things that cannot exist independently of being perceived.

THE NATURE OF SENSIBLE THINGS

Hylas and Philonous have so far been in happy agreement on the nature of the sensible. This quickly changes when they come to consider whether sensible things are nothing but ideas.

> P: Doth the reality of sensible things consist in being perceived? Or, is it something distinct from their being perceived, and that bears no relation to the mind?
>
> H: To *exist* is one thing, and to be *perceived* is another.
>
> P: I speak with regard to sensible things only: and of these I ask, whether by their real existence you mean a subsistence exterior to the mind, and distinct from their being perceived?
>
> H: I mean a real absolute being, distinct from, and without any relation to their being perceived. (175)

Hylas states quite categorically that he takes sensible things to exist wholly distinct from being perceived. Since they have agreed that sensible things are what is immediately perceived by sense, and that what is perceived in such a way is sensible qualities, namely light, colours, sounds, tastes, odours and tangible qualities, it follows that, according to Hylas, these sensible qualities exist without any relation to their being perceived. Much of the remainder of the dialogue involves Philonous trying to convince Hylas that he is mistaken and that the reality of sensible things consists only in their being perceived.

IS HEAT MIND-DEPENDENT? A CASE STUDY IN PHILONOUS' ARGUMENTATIVE STRATEGY

Throughout the first dialogue Philonous chiefly employs two forms of arguments to convince Hylas that sensible qualities are mind-dependent. Commentators have given these forms of argument a number of labels over the years. I will follow Stoneham's (2002: 62) nicely descriptive terms and refer to them as the 'assimilation' argument and the 'conflicting appearance' argument. My presentation of these arguments is broadly in agreement with Muehlmann (1992) and Rickless (2013) in seeing the 'assimilation' argument as a direct argument for the mind-dependence of sensible qualities and the 'conflicting appearances' argument as an indirect argument aimed at revealing problems with materialism.

The first sensible quality that they discuss is 'heat'. It is no coincidence that Berkeley begins his discussion with this sensible quality. Many materialist philosophers would accept that heat is mind-dependent, and by letting the discussion begin with Hylas defending the mind-independence of this quality, Berkeley makes Hylas embody materialism in its most extreme, and perhaps least convincing, form. Heat seems to be a sensible quality, and, on Hylas' view, it must exist independently of being perceived. Heat must be a quality that exists in external objects, such as a fire. Philonous quickly levels a challenge to this view by presenting a line of thought that concludes that heat can only exist in the mind. This is his first application of the 'assimilation' argument:

P: But is not the most vehement and intense degree of heat a very great pain?

H: No one can deny it.

P: And is any unperceiving thing capable of pain or pleasure?

H: No certainly.

P: Is your material substance a sensible being, or a being endowed with sense and perception?

H: It is senseless, without a doubt.

P: It cannot therefore be the subject of pain.

H: By no means.

P: Nor consequently of the greatest heat perceived by sense, as you acknowledge this to be no small pain.

> H: I grant it.
> P: What shall we say then of your external object; is it a material substance, or no?
> H: It is a material substance with the sensible qualities inhering in it.
> P: How then can a great heat exist in it, since you own it cannot in a material substance? I desire you would clear this point. (176)

It is worth looking at this exchange in some detail as it is the starting point for the whole discussion of the nature of sensible qualities. Philonous makes two central claims that Hylas quickly, too quickly as it turns out, accepts. The first point they agree on is that a very strong degree of heat is identical to pain. In other words, when one feels a vehement degree of heat there are not two sensations, one of heat and one of pain, but only one sensation. The second point is that pain is a purely subjective experience that does not exist in any object anywhere in the external world. Once Hylas has agreed on these two points he gets into trouble. If extreme heat is identical to pain and pain is a purely subjective sensation that cannot exist in any external object, it follows that extreme heat is equally subjective. It is, therefore, impossible for extreme heat to exist in an external object, such as a fire. The point of this argument is to *assimilate* the sensible quality of extreme heat to something that is undoubtedly mind-dependent, in this case pain.

A straightforward way to respond to this argument would be for Hylas to challenge either of the two points agreed on. He can either defend the view that extreme heat and pain are different sensations, or he can argue that pain is not a purely subjective experience. If he goes down the second route, then he is committed to the view that 'pain' exists in certain unthinking things, perhaps in a fire. This is something that he is not prepared to defend at this point, and as it seems to be such an outlandish claim it is easy to understand why. Instead, he goes down the first route:

> H: Hold, Philonous, I fear I was out in yielding intense heat to be a pain. It should seem rather, that pain is something distinct from heat, and the consequence or effect of it.
> P: Upon putting your hand near the fire, do you perceive one simple uniform sensation, or two distinct sensations?
> H: But one simple sensation.

P: Is not the heat immediately perceived?

H: It is.

P: And the pain?

H: True.

P: Seeing therefore they are both immediately perceived at the
      same time, and the fire affects you only with one simple or
      uncompounded idea, it follows that this same simple idea is
      both the intense heat immediately perceived and the pain; and
      consequently, that the intense heat immediately perceived is
      nothing distinct from a particular sort of pain.

H: It seems so. (176)

Hylas states that pain is distinct from extreme heat, specifically, it is
a consequence or effect of it. Philonous responds by presenting an
argument opposed to this claim, which Hylas accepts. Philonous'
argument concerns our own experience of feeling something very
hot. Again, Philonous' argument depends on two crucial claims.
First, that the sensation of intense heat and the sensation of pain do
not follow one after the other. Rather, I feel both sensations at the
same time. Second, when I touch something very hot, for example,
when I put my hand in a fire and I feel the extreme heat and the pain
(which they agree, are sensed at the same time), there is no qualitative
difference between the intense heat and the pain. Therefore, as there
is no temporal or qualitative difference between what I describe as
'intense heat' and what I describe as 'pain', I feel only one sensation
which is best described as a particular sort of pain. Philonous is here
appealing to the phenomenology of pain. His point is that in those
cases in which I sense a burning heat, there is no additional distinct
sensation of pain, it is the burning sensation itself that is the pain. Is
this plausible? One reason to think that it is, is that the sensation of
extreme heat as pain and the sensation of intense cold as pain seem to
be indistinguishable, at least in certain cases. If someone puts an ice
cube against the skin of a blindfolded person, that person typically
believes that she has been burned. This should not be the case if heat
had its own what-it-is-likeness that is phenomenologically different
from the sensation of pain.

Hylas has no further objection to the claim that intense heat and
a particular kind of pain are the same sensible quality. However,

three issues seem to arise quite naturally from this exchange. First, it might seem false to say that we sense the extreme heat and the pain at the same time, because in a case in which we approach a fire we first sense a moderate, increasing heat and only when our hand is very close to the fire do we sense pain. However, Philonous only states that *intense* heat is sensed at the same time as the pain. When our hand approaches the fire we sense moderate heat, and, as we shall soon see, Philonous does not think that sensation is painful at all, but rather pleasurable. Therefore, while it is true that we sense moderate heat before pain in our example, that fact does not invalidate Philonous' claim about intense heat.

Second, we might want to object against the identification of extreme heat and pain on the grounds that sometimes when we experience intense heat we do not experience pain. If we are under a powerful anaesthetic, for example, we could put our hand close to, or even in, the fire without experiencing any pain. We might see damage to the hand, smell burnt flesh, perhaps even feel a small degree of pressure on our hand as the flames touches it. But here we must ask if we actually *sense* any intense heat. Smelling burnt flesh and all the rest is not a direct sensation of heat, but requires intermediate inference or association. While most of us would not want to try this theory out ourselves there are some people who cannot feel pain because they suffer from congenital insensitivity to pain as a result of a genetic mutation that results in the deactivation of all pain sensors in the body from birth. These people report that they cannot feel heat, even if they put their hand in boiling water.

Third, if we agree with Philonous that extreme heat is identical to a kind of pain, it might seem to have strange consequences for how we understand the nature of sensible objects. Our two protagonists have not said much about what sensible objects are. They have agreed that they are composed of sensible qualities, and Hylas has, in addition, stated that on his view sensible qualities inhere in mind-independent material substance. If sensible objects are composed of sensible qualities and intense heat is a sensible quality, which is identical to a certain kind of pain, then pain is also a sensible quality and is part of a sensible object. But this commits us to the strange-sounding claim that the pain is in the fire. Why is this strange? If we, with Hylas, hold that sensible qualities inhere in material substances, then it follows that a seemingly purely subjective experience inheres in an unperceiving object. This is not only strange but seems incoherent because the substance must be both unperceiving (because it is material) and perceiving (because pain inheres in it) at the same time.

Philonous, who does not accept the existence of material substance, will not be faced with that particular problem. On his view sensible objects are composed of mind-dependent sensible qualities, therefore, he has no issue with such objects being composed of purely subjective sensations. Nonetheless, it does seem strange to say that pain is in the fire. We will have to assess Philonous' conception of sensible objects more fully at a later point (Chapter 7) and see if this apparent strangeness persists.

At this point in the dialogue Hylas is convinced that an intense heat is identical to a particular kind of pain and therefore that intense heat cannot exist in a sensible thing, understood as a material substance. He must, therefore, ban intense heat from the realm of real things that exists in physical objects and so he must hold that, in reality, fire is not intensely hot. But, what about moderate heat or warmth? Hylas now tries to argue that a sensible quality of this sort can exist in a sensible object, understood as a material substance.

> H: [B]ecause intense heat is nothing else but a particular kind of painful sensation, and pain cannot exist but in a perceiving being, it follows that no intense heat can really exist in an unperceiving corporeal substance. But this is no reason why we should deny heat in an inferior degree to exist in such a substance.

Hylas' reason for stating that warmth, as opposed to intense heat, can exist in sensible objects is that warmth is not bound up with the sensation of pain. In response to this Philonous states:

> P: I think you granted before, that no unperceiving being was capable of pleasure, any more than of pain.
> H: I did.
> P: And is not warmth, or a more gentle degree of heat than what causes uneasiness, a pleasure?
> H: What then?

> *P:* Consequently it cannot exist without the mind in any perceiving
> substance, or body.
>
> *H:* So it seems. (177)

Philonous' approach to warmth (understood as less warm than intense heat) is to state that it is a kind of pleasurable sensation. Further, just as pain is a mind-dependent sensation, so too is pleasure. Philonous presumably has in mind such things as the gentle warmth perceived while sitting by an open fire or when holding a cup of warm tea. At this point Hylas could object that sometimes a moderate warmth is painful. To be in stifling heat is to have a sensation of heat that is significantly less than that when one's hand is in a fire, yet it is typically unpleasant and, therefore, painful to some extent. There is no reason why Philonous would not accept this. His view is simply that sensations of heat and cold are identical to sensations of pain and pleasure and, therefore, are mind-dependent. This is compatible with the same degree of heat causing one to feel pleasure at one point in time and pain or discomfort at another point in time. Instead, Hylas approaches the issue in a different way:

> *H:* On second thoughts, I do not think it so evident that warmth is
> a pleasure, as that a great degree of heat is a pain.
>
> *P:* I do not pretend that warmth is as great a pleasure as heat is a
> pain. But if you grant it to be even a small pleasure, it serves to
> make good my conclusion.
>
> *H:* I could rather call it an indolence. It seems to be nothing more
> than a privation of both pain and pleasure. (178)

Hylas' first response is to state that there is a qualitative difference between the pain of intense heat and the pleasure of moderate warmth. Philonous retorts that this is beside the point. His claim is not that the pain and pleasure are equal in intensity but that they are equally identified with pain or pleasure, regardless of the degree. At this point Hylas challenges the identification of warmth and pleasure, stating that a moderate degree of warmth is neither pain nor pleasure. If Hylas is right here, then the objection is on the mark and Philonous cannot maintain the mind-dependence of heat through the identification of those sensations with pain and pleasure. Why think that a moderate degree of warmth is neither painful nor pleasurable? We can imagine a situation in which there is a subtle change in temperature of a room such that the temperature rise by one degree and that, in such a situation, neither pain nor pleasure is experienced by those in the room. However, this case is beside the point. Philonous' claim is not that every measurable *change of temperature* is identical to pain or pleasure, but that every *sensation* of a different temperature is thus associated with pain or pleasure. If a change of temperature is so small that one does not sense it, there is, accordingly, no requirement that one feels pain or pleasure.

Hylas digs in his heels here, and holds fast with his conviction that intense heat is pain and therefore, in the mind, but moderate heat is neither pain nor pleasure and, therefore, should be allowed to exist in material objects. This seems like a strange position for Hylas to maintain. It would be more sensible to let all degrees of perceived heat be either in the object or in the subject. Instead, his current view suggests that if one puts a cold iron in the fire, it first has the mind-independent quality of mild coldness, then the equally mind-independent quality of warmness, but then suddenly when it gets very hot, it loses its temperature quality and extreme heat is not in the iron, but only in the mind of the perceiver. This leaves Philonous exasperated: "If you are resolved to maintain that warmth, or a gentle degree of heat, is no pleasure, I know not how to convince you otherwise than by appealing to your own sense" (178).

Philonous has one further argument against the mind-independence of heat and cold, the 'conflicting appearances' argument. Hylas believes that sensible objects possess the sensible qualities we sense in them, just to the degree they are sensed (175–6, 178). Hylas is assuming a straightforward connection between what material things are like on the basis of our sensory awareness of them. We believe that tomatoes are red because we see them as red, wormwood is bitter because it tastes bitter to us, and so on. Likewise, Hylas believes that if something is felt to be moderately warm or cold, then it possesses the quality of moderate warmness or coldness. Philonous argument is a *reductio ad absurdum* of Hylas' view that sensible qualities, as we sense them, exist in material objects. In other words, Philonous' argument assumes that Hylas' view is correct and then shows that an absurdity follows if the view is granted:

P: Can any doctrine be true that necessarily leads a man into an absurdity?

H: Without a doubt it cannot.

P: Is it not an absurdity to think that the same thing should be at the same time both cold and warm?

H: It is. (178)

Hylas agrees on the validity of an argument from absurdity and agrees on a relevant criterion for an absurdity, sometimes referred to as a consistency principle, that the same thing cannot be both hot and cold at the same time. For the principle to be valid some qualifications will of course be necessary. Many things are both hot and cold at the same time. The earth is cold at the poles and warm around the equator. When our protagonists agree on the principles we should therefore assume that they are speaking of medium sized objects under normal circumstances.

The argument is presented in the following way:

P: Suppose now one of your hands hot, and the other cold, and that they are both at once put into the same vessel of water, in an intermediate state; will not the water seem cold to one hand, and warm to the other?

H: It will.

P: Ought we not therefore by your principles to conclude, it is really both cold and warm at the same time, that is, according to your own concession, to believe an absurdity.

H: I confess it seems so.

P: Consequently, the principles themselves are false, since you have granted that no true principle leads to an absurdity. (178–9)

The argument has the following structure. First, assume, with Hylas, that sensible things are mind-independent objects and that sensible things are just as we perceive them to be. Second, if we put one of our hands, which is hot, and the other, which is cold, into a vat of lukewarm water, we will feel the water to be, at the same time, both warm and cold. Furthermore, since we have assumed that things are just as they are sensed to be, it follows that the material substance, the water, really is both warm and cold at the same time. This conclusion, however, is absurd, so the principles that led to it, namely, either the principle that sensible things are the way they are directly senses, or the principle that sensible things are mind-independent, must be rejected. It is the *conflicting appearances* of sensible things that generate this problem.

How can Hylas get out of this bind? He has a number of routes open to him. Let us first consider the second step of the argument. Hylas and Philonous agree that if you put a warm and a cold hand in lukewarm water, the water will feel both warm and cold. This is a common assumption, for example, we find it in classical works such as Locke's *Essay* (2.8.21) and Titchener's *Text-Book of Psychology* (1909–10). But is this true? You should really try it yourself! David Berman, in his *A Manual of Experimental Philosophy* (2009) presents reports from a number of people who have conducted a version of the experiment in which the test subject first has both hands in lukewarm water and then places each hand in a separate bowl that is warm and cold respectively. To avoid stimulus error, the participants did not know beforehand which bowl had warm water and which had cold. The results were mixed. Some participants reported that one hand sensed the water as warm and the other sensed it as cold. But other participants had different experiences. One test subject reported: "The body of water feels the same temperature to both hands" (p. 48) and instead reports "glowing" and "stinging" sensations. Berman himself similarly reports that his left hand often feels a "strange and tinge-ing" sensation whereas the right hand senses in the way predicted by Hylas and Philonous. However, this does not point to a clear rebuttal for Hylas. As long as some people feel the water to be both hot and cold at the same time, it is the case that for some people there is an experiential situation that is inexplicable on Hylas' assumptions.

Let us instead consider the first premise of the argument, that material objects are sensible things that have the qualities they are perceived to have. This is really a compound of two separable positions. On the one hand, there is the belief in the existence of material substance, and, on the other hand, the common sense belief about the veracity of our perceptual experience. Hylas is committed to both views but as the dialogue progresses, he is made to choose between the two. Because he doesn't want to give up on materialism, he is made to discard his common sense intuitions and to move towards a materialism marred by scepticism. This is ultimately Berkeley's intention. He wants to prize apart these two components and argue that materialism is antithetical to common sense. In this way, Hylas' response to all of Philonous' arguments in the first dialogue is to deny that material sensible objects have the properties we perceive them to have. But is it really a concession for Hylas to admit that not all sensible qualities are in objects?

If he can accept this, then he can say that there really is a way in which the material substance, the water, is, namely, lukewarm, but that in this instance he is *mistaken* when his hands feel the water to be both hot and cold. Unfortunately for Hylas, he does not think of this objection at this point, though he will soon raise this point as we will see in Chapter 4. Instead he accepts that the same thing can be sensed as having different temperatures at the same time, and that sensible, material objects cannot have inconsistent properties, that the various temperatures that we feel are not part of the sensible, material object. This pushes Hylas towards scepticism, as he himself notes: "But after all, can anything be more absurd than to say, *there is no heat in the fire*?" (179). With this Hylas abandons the idea that temperature, in all its degrees, is a mind-independent property. But he is still hopeful for "there still remains qualities enough to secure the reality of external things" (179).

TASTE, SMELL AND SOUNDS: HYLAS' HOBBESIAN APPROACH

After his success with heat and cold, Philonous quickly applies the 'assimilation' and 'conflicting appearances' arguments to the qualities of tastes, smells, and sounds. With regard to the first two kinds of qualities, Hylas concedes, rather meekly, that they are mind-dependent. As with heat and cold, these sensible qualities, Hylas accepts, are so closely woven in with the feelings of pain and pleasure as to really be identical with them. Further, they are so dependent on the observer that they appear to be merely subjective. Philonous states the 'assimilation' argument for tastes in the following way:

P: What think you of tastes, do they exist without the mind, or no?

H: Can any man in his senses doubt whether sugar is sweet, or wormwood bitter?

P: Inform me, Hylas. Is a sweet taste a particular kind of pleasure or pleasant sensation, or is it not?

H: It is.

P: And is not bitterness some kind of uneasiness or pain?

H: I grant it. (179–80)

The 'conflicting appearances' argument for tastes is equally brief:

P: That which at other times seems sweet, shall to a distempered palate appear bitter. And nothing can be plainer, than that divers persons perceive different tastes in the same food, since that which one man delights in, another abhors. And how could this be, if the taste was something really inherent in the food?

H: I acknowledge I know not how. (180)

Likewise with smells:

P: And with regard to these [odours], I would fain know, whether what hath been said of tastes doth not exactly agree to them? Are they not so many pleasing or displeasing sensations?

H: They are.

P: Can you then conceive it possible that they should exist in an unperceiving thing?

H: I cannot.

P: Or can you imagine, that filth and ordure affect those brute animals that feed on them out of choice, with the same smells which we perceive in them?

H: By no means.

P: May we not therefore conclude of smells, as of the other forementioned qualities, that they cannot exist in any but a perceiving substance or mind?

H: I think so. (180–1)

Hylas does make one noteworthy move when they discuss the 'assimilation' argument for tastes. He now thinks he has hit on a way to distinguish between temperature and taste, on the one hand, and pain and pleasure, on the other. This approach is, as Lisa Downing (2018: 18) has pointed out, a doctrine of "double existence". It is true, he states, that in *one sense* words like 'cold' or 'sweet' are just certain pains and pleasures, but in *another sense* these words stand for something else. If by 'cold' and 'sweet' we mean those qualities that are perceived by us and that are in our mind, then yes they are nothing but different degrees of pain and pleasure. If, however, we also hold that there is another set of qualities with the same names, which are in the objects themselves, then we can say that heat is in fire and that bitterness is in the wormwood. That is, we can conserve our commonsensical way of speaking of the relation between sensible qualities and sensible objects, while maintaining a materialist conception of the latter.

Here Hylas is presenting the view of the influential British philosopher Thomas Hobbes. He stated: "the *heat* we feel from the fire is manifestly in *us*, and is quite *different* from the heat which is in the *fire*: for *our* heat is *pleasure* or *pain* according as it is *great* or *moderate*: but in the *coal* there is no such thing" (1652: 7). In other words, Hobbes distinguished between two conceptions of heat. One notion of heat is "in us", this is heat understood as being identical to either pain or pleasure, which he assumed was mind-dependent. But he also stated that there is another kind of heat, which is not identical to pain and pleasure, which exists solely in the material object (such as a hot iron or a fire). Hylas seems to be assuming a similar model of heat and other qualities in objects.

Philonous' reply here is simple. Sensible qualities, they have agreed, are those that are immediately perceived by our senses. The question, at present, is whether *these* qualities are mind-dependent or not. Hylas has posited another, completely different, set of qualities. Thus, as Hylas has stated his objection it is irrelevant to the question at hand. This reply by Philonous is rather quick. Hylas has not specified what these qualities are (besides the merely negative account he has given). They might conceivably be related (perhaps causally) to the sensible qualities and therefore, perhaps, germane to the discussion. Hylas temporarily gives up the point because he does not yet have an adequate account of what this second set of mind-independent qualities could be. This might be because he has no informative scientific theory about how tastes are related to other aspects of physical objects.

Whatever the reason for Hylas' capitulation here, when they turn to sound Hylas returns to this Hobbesian materialist solution largely because with regard to sound he *does* have a scientific account of how different aspects of, and conditions for, sound are related. Philonous begins the discussion by asking whether sound is a quality that exists in mind-independent objects. Hylas gives a rather specific answer. Clearly he has done his reading on the latest scientific research, in particular, he is familiar with the leading Irish scientist Robert Boyle's *New Experiments Physico-Mechanical, Touching the Spring of the Air, and its Effects* (1660). Boyle, together with the English scientist Robert Hooke, had developed an efficient vacuum pump. Boyle put a ringing bell inside a container and successively removed all air from it. The sound of the bell became more and more faint until no sound was heard. He concluded that sound requires the medium of air. Here is Hylas' take on these experimental findings:

> P: Then as to sounds, what must we think of them: are they accidents really inherent in external bodies or not?
>
> H: That they inhere not in the sonorous bodies is plain from hence: because a bell struck in the exhausted receiver of an air-pump sends forth no sound. The air therefore must be thought the subject of sound.
>
> P: What reason is there for that, Hylas?
>
> H: Because when any motion is raised in the air, we perceive a sound greater or lesser, in proportion to the air's motion; but without some motion in the air, we never hear any sound at all. (181)

According to Hylas, the sensible quality of sound exists independently of the mind. But he does not think that sounds exist in sensible objects like bells or clarinets. Instead he claims that sound exists in the air, on the basis of the experimental evidence of Boyle's air pump. Hylas accordingly draws a philosophical conclusion about the nature of the sensible quality of sound from a scientific experiment. Philonous does not dispute the scientific findings, but he does not think that the inference is warranted. As Philonous immediately points out, just because no sound is ever heard without motion in the air, it does not immediately follow that the sound itself is in the air. After all, Hylas has accepted that heat is not in the fire, even though he accepts that we feel heat when we are near a fire. Hylas continues with his scientific explanation by giving a causal account of how the movement of the air affects our senses:

> H: It is this very motion in the external air that produces in the mind the sensation of sound. For, striking on the drum of the ear, it causes a vibration, which by the auditory nerves being communicated to the brain, the soul is thereupon affected with the sensation called 'sound'. (181)

As Hylas presents his view here, the sensation called 'sound' is the sensible *effect* of the movement of the air, not strictly the movement of the air itself. Philonous pounces on this opportunity.

> P: What! Is sound then a sensation?
> H: I tell you, as perceived by us, it is a particular sensation in the mind.
> P: And can any sensation exist without the mind?
> H: No certainly.
> P: How then can sound, being a sensation, exist in the air, if by the 'air' you mean a senseless substance existing without the mind?
> H: You must distinguish, Philonous, between sound as it is perceived by us, and as it is in itself; or (which is the same thing) between the sound we immediately perceive and that which exists without us. The former indeed is a particular kind of sensation, but the latter is merely a vibrative or undulatory [having the form of a wave] motion in the air. (181–2)

Hylas again tries out the doctrine of double existence. In one sense of the word, 'sound' signifies a sensation that exist only in the mind. In another sense the word 'sound' means "a vibrative or undulatory motion in the air". Philonous' reply this time is different. We saw with the case of temperature and smells that he relied on their shared view of what a sensible quality is; but this time he questions Hylas' semantic propriety.

P: are you sure then that sound is really nothing but motion?

H: I am.

P: Whatever therefore agrees to real sound, may with truth be attributed to motion.

H: It may.

P: It is then good sense to speak of motion, as of a thing that is loud, sweet, acute, or grave.

H: I see you are resolved not to understand me. Is it not evident, those accidents or modes belong only to sensible sound, or sound in the common acceptation of the word, but not to sound in the real and philosophic sense, which, as I just now told you, is nothing but a certain motion of the air?

P: It seems then there are two sorts of sound, the one vulgar, or that which is heard, the other philosophical and real.

H: Even so.

P: And the latter consists in motion.

H: I told you so before.

P: Tell me, Hylas, to which of the senses, think you, the idea of motion belongs: to the hearing?

H: No certainly, but to the sight and touch.

P: It should follow then that, according to you, real sounds may possibly be seen or felt, but never heard.

There are two steps to Philonous' argument here. First, Hylas states that in the version of double existence now under consideration the two senses of the word 'sound' are not on equal footing. One conception of sound is the 'real' and 'philosophical' or, as we would say today, 'scientific' notion of the movement of the air. The other conception is the 'vulgar', meaning 'common' and 'uneducated', namely, the sensation of sound. Second, given that the 'real' notion of sound is a kind of motion, Philonous asks how we get to know about this motion. Hylas states that motion is perceived by the senses of sight and touch. Therefore, it seems that 'real' sound can be seen and felt by touch, but not heard.

Hylas' first reaction to this is to accept the peculiar 'real' or 'scientific' understanding of the word 'sound'. His reason is that what he calls "common language" (182) is imprecise, and that the exact philosophical truth in this instance is contrary to common language and opinion.

Philonous immediately seizes on this opportunity to remind Hylas that they have agreed that a central criterion of the better theory about the nature of sensible things is that the theory is commensurate with common sense. Now Hylas is committing himself to claims such as "real sounds are never heard" (183). In the face of this objection Hylas gives up and agrees with Philonous that sounds have no real being without the mind. Though this is not made explicit in the text, this presumably means that Hylas rejects the idea that there is a conception of sound that is distinct from the sensation of sound.

IS COLOUR MIND-DEPENDENT? IN SEARCH OF
A CRITERION OF TRUTH

The discussion of the nature of colour in the *Three Dialogues* is one of the most widely debated issues in Berkeley scholarship. It has, moreover, remained influential in debates about the nature of colour for centuries, and is still considered to be a discussion that must be addressed, even if one does not agree with the conclusion.[1] At this point in the dialogue the protagonists, as well as the readers, are supposed to be attuned to the various assumptions, strategies, arguments and counter-arguments that have entered into the discussions of temperature, taste, smell and sound. The discussion of colour, therefore, represents the culmination of the discussion up to this point and the philosophical sophistication is successively ramped up.

We have seen that the dialectic has the following movement: Hylas states that sensible qualities, as they are immediately perceived, inhere in either physical objects, or a medium such as air, which itself is understood to be a material substance. At some points Philonous argues that the sensible quality is identical with a kind of pain or pleasure. This argument has mixed results on Hylas who sometimes agrees and sometimes disagrees, stating that introspection reveals to him that certain sensible qualities are indifferent with respect to pain and pleasure.

Another argument that Philonous uses concerns perceptual variability. This consists in Philonous pointing out that things are perceived to have different sensible qualities, by different people at the same time, by the same person at different times, and sometimes even by the same person at the same time (as in the bucket of water example). If the sensible qualities we perceive are always found in the objects, as they are perceived, then it follows that sensible objects have contradictory properties such as being both hot and cold, or bitter and sweet, at the same time. Let's call this the 'metaphysical' application of the conflicting appearances argument. The point of the argument is that Hylas will end up asserting that material substance is composed of contradictory properties such as being both warm and cold in the same respect at the same time.

The unpleasant consequences of the metaphysical argument lead Hylas to refine his commitment to the view that we always perceive the sensible qualities that pertain to a sensible object by distinguishing between real and apparent instances of the sensible quality, the doctrine of double existence. Through Philonous' prodding on this distinction, Hylas is made to state that the real instances of the sensible quality are not as a sensation of the relevant sense modality but, if a sensation at all, then a sensation belonging to some other sense. In the case of sounds Hylas accepts that real sound is a motion of the air and so can be sensed by touch but not by hearing. Philonous then points out the non-commonsensical nature of Hylas' position at which point he capitulates and accepts that the relevant sensation is mind-dependent. This is the 'common sense' application of the argument from perceptual relativity.

The discussion of colour is, again, a discussion about true and apparent sensible qualities. Here Philonous raises the issue of whether, and if so how, it makes sense to draw the real/apparent distinction between instances of sensations of the same kind, in the case of colours this is, of course, visual sensations. This leads the discussion to how to understand veridical experience in general and the criterion of truth in experience. Philonous leads Hylas to distinguish between real and apparent colour in the following way:

> P: Only be pleased to let me know whether the same colours which we see, exist in external bodies, or some other.
>
> H: The very same.
>
> P: What! are then the beautiful red and purple we see on yonder clouds, really in them? Or do you imagine they have in themselves any other form, than that of a dark mist or vapour?
>
> H: I must own, Philonous, those colours are not really in the clouds as they seem to be at this distance. They are only apparent colours.
>
> P: 'Apparent' call you them? how shall we distinguish these apparent colours from real? (184)

The clouds above them look red and purple from where they are standing, but if they were closer to them Hylas thinks that they would look like dark mist. He therefore says that the red and purple colours do not really belong to the clouds but are the merely apparent colours of the clouds. Presumably the grey misty look perceived on closer inspection is the true colour. Philonous continues by suggesting a criterion for determining what the true colour of objects is, which Hylas immediately accepts:

P: And those I suppose are to be thought real, which are discovered by the most near and exact survey.
H: Right. (184)

Philonous takes the distinction between real and apparent colours to concern an ideal viewing condition. If someone looks at an object in certain conditions, then the true colour will be manifest. If the object is viewed in less favourable conditions, a merely apparent colour is seen. The criterion in question could be said to be 'acuity' as it is a matter of seeing something "near and exact". But what does "near and exact" mean in this case? They both agree that things are more nearly and exactly viewed through a microscope than with the naked eye. At this point Philonous is ready to start attacking Hylas' position:

P: But a microscope often discovers colours in an object different from those perceived by the unassisted sight. And in case we had microscopes magnifying to an assigned degree, it is certain that no object whatsoever, viewed through them, would appear in the same colour which it exhibits to the naked eye.
H: And what will you conclude from all this? You cannot argue that there are really and naturally no colours on objects because, by artificial managements, they may be altered or made to vanish.
P: I think it may evidently be concluded, from your own concessions, that all the colours we see with our naked eyes are only apparent as those on the clouds, since they vanish upon a more close and accurate inspection, which is afforded us by a microscope. (184–5)

If acuity is the criterion for distinguishing true from apparent colour, and microscopes offer better acuity, and colours look different (or disappear altogether) when an object is viewed through a microscope, then everything viewed by the naked eye is merely apparent colour. This effect of microscopes was well known at the time. Locke, in the *Essay*, makes the point that blood looks red to the naked eye, but when viewed in a microscope one finds red particles interspersed in a translucent liquid (*Essay* 2.23.11). Such a conclusion might worry Hylas because he can see how Philonous could draw non-commonsensical conclusions from this. Namely that grass is not green, blood is not red and so forth. But Hylas might accept this because in this case the situation is different from the case of for example sound. In that case Hylas was made to state a view contrary to common sense because real sound is never heard. In this case real colour can be seen, it is just that it requires an instrument to see the correct colour. However, this is not the direction that Philonous wants to take his objection:

P: What think you of those inconceivably small animals perceived by glasses? Must we suppose they are all stark blind? Or, in case they see, can it be imagined their sight has not the same use in preserving their bodies from injuries, which appears in that of all other animals? And if it has, is it not evident, they must see particles less than their own bodies, which will present them with a far different view in each object, from that which strikes our senses? [. . .] Is it not therefore highly probable, those animals in whose eyes we discern a very different texture from that of ours and whose bodies abound with different humours, do not see the same colours in every object that we do? From all which should it not seem to follow, that all colours are equally apparent, and that none of those which we perceive are really inherent in any outward object?

H: It should. (185–6)

Philonous' aim here is to further undermine Hylas' distinction between real and apparent colours. He first says that it is probable that small animals like mites can see colours in a sense roughly analogous to the way we do. As they are so small, it is certain that their vision is adapted to see very small things that our naked eye could not see. When they look at a region of an object, the colour they see will therefore most probably be different from the colour we see. Further, as Margaret Wilson (1987) has pointed out, Philonous appeals to certain scientific considerations to further undermine Hylas' distinction between real and apparent colours. Animals differ from us not just in size, but they also have differences in their visual structure ("texture") and also manifest biochemical differences ("humours") which might indicate different visual sensations. For example, animals with compound eyes might see things radically differently from the way we do, and animals that are visually sensitive to ultraviolet radiation would also have radically different visual experience than we do.

We might say that we have good reason to take normal human sight as our standard, after all, that is what the colour words were designed to pick out. For example, we think that someone who is colour blind sees things in a defective way. While we could draw a distinction between real and apparent colour along the line of common human sight, that would not establish Hylas' point that the 'true' colours are mind-independent. If Hylas thinks that true colour just is common human perception in ideal conditions, he then has to make the further point that the distinction between real and apparent colour maps on to the distinction between mind-independent colour and mind-dependent sensation. It is hard to see how this can be done. To return to the contrast with the bee, the bee is not colour blind, it is a radically different animal, that, when functioning normally (for a bee) perceives colour very differently from humans. Here there is no reason to think that the criterion for true colour perception, the normally functioning human visual system, as opposed to, say, that of the normally functioning bee, is the relevant non-arbitrary situation. Therefore, there is no reason to think that our perceptual apparatus discerns the mind-independent colour that is really on the object while the bee's does not. Since Hylas' theory requires that true and apparent colour sensation refers to an external object, but that it is impossible in each case to know what the true colour is, all colour is equally apparent. For him every perceptual situation is just like the purple cloud scenario. As Philonous puts it:

> P: And now tell me, whether you [Hylas] are still of opinion that every body has its true real colour inhering in it; and if you think it has, I would fain know farther from you, what certain distance and position of the object, what peculiar texture and formation of the eye, what degree or kind of light is necessary for ascertaining that true colour and distinguishing it from apparent ones. (186)

The conflicting appearances argument is here put to use in a different way from the case of sound. In the case of sound, Hylas' distinction between true sound as motion and apparent sound as something heard, led him to accept that the distinction, thus construed, was contrary to common sense. In the case of colour, Hylas is not appealing to something outside our sensation as the true colour. His problem is instead one of finding the criterion by which he may distinguish the true from the apparent. His inability to solve this problem puts him in a position that is, in a sense, worse than his position with respect to sound. In the case of sound, he *did* have a criterion for distinguishing the true from the apparent, though the true sounds are hardly sounds. If he pins his hopes on distinguishing true and apparent colours to cases of true perception of sensible colours of objects, he simply has no way of knowing whether he is seeing the true or the apparent colour, because he has admitted that he cannot present a criterion of truth. Therefore, he cannot determine if he is right or wrong, if he is seeing a real colour or an illusionary colour. Hylas is now wading deeply into the scepticism he abhors. This is the 'sceptical' application of the argument from conflicting appearances.

In the face of this difficulty Hylas reverts to a double existence theory of colour according to which true colour is in 'light' and apparent colour is in the mind, whereas there is no colour in the objects themselves.

> *H:* I tell you, Philonous, external light is nothing but a thin fluid substance whose minute particles, being agitated with a brisk motion and in various manners reflected from the different surfaces of outward objects to the eyes, communicate different motions to the optic nerves; which, being propagated to the brain, cause therein various impressions, and these are attended with the sensations of red, blue, yellow, &c.
>
> *P:* It seems, then, the light does no more than shake the optic nerves.
>
> *H:* Nothing else.
>
> *P:* And consequent to each particular motion of the nerves the mind is affected with a sensation, which is some particular colour.
>
> *H:* Right.
>
> *P:* And these sensations have no existence without the mind.

H: They have not.

P: How then do you affirm that colours are in the light, since by 'light' you understand a corporeal substance external to the mind?

H: Light and colours, as immediately perceived by us, I grant cannot exist without the mind. But in themselves they are only the motions and configurations of certain insensible particles of matter.

P: Colours then, in the vulgar sense, or taken for the immediate objects of sight, cannot agree to any but a perceiving substance.

H: That is what I say.

P: Well then, since you give up the point as to those sensible qualities, which are alone thought colours by all mankind beside, you may hold what you please with regard to those invisible ones of the philosophers. It is not my business to dispute about them; only I would advise you to bethink yourself, whether considering the inquiry we are upon, it be prudent for you to affirm 'the red and blue which we see are not real colours, but certain unknown motions and figures which no man ever did or can see are truly so.' Are not these shocking notions, and are not they subject to as many ridiculous inferences, as those you were obliged to renounce before in the case of sounds? (187)

Hylas' description of the nature of light in his first statement in the above passage is interesting. While Hylas often appeals to the standard scientific theories of his time in his answers to Philonous, the view he presents here is more idiosyncratic. Further, it is a controversial theory that Berkeley himself would later make a major contribution to in *Siris*, though he would do so within the framework of his immaterialist metaphysics, as opposed to Hylas' explicitly materialist position here. The main theoretical approach to the nature of light in Britain and Ireland at the time was the class of so-called 'projectile' theories of light developed in Molyneux's *Dioptrica Nova* (1692) and, more famously in Newton's *Optics* (1704). It sought to reduce optics to a branch of particle dynamics by treating rays of light as streams of rapidly moving particles or 'corpuscles' moving in accordance with the Newtonian laws of motion. The main rival class of theories were the 'wave' and 'vibration' theories that saw light as analogous to sound, promoted by, among others, Malebranche *Search* (Elucidation 16) and Christiaan Huygens *Treatise on Light* (1690), Though Hylas' summary of 'his' position is brief, it seems clear that Hylas is stating neither of these positions but the lesser known 'fluid' theory of light that proudly tracks its lineage to Neoplatonists and Hermetic writers of the Renaissance, and had its most famous expression in John Hutchinson's extraordinary *Moses Principia, Part I* (1724) and Hermann Boerhaave's *A New Method of Chemistry* (1727). On this view rays of light are understood as fast-moving currents of particles in a ubiquitous aetherial medium, and they were typically given immaterial and even divine properties. Berkeley's reference to this theory as early as 1713 should be of interest to historiographers of theories of light, but the details need not concern us any further here.[2]

Besides the exotic nature of the theory of light, the discussion that follows is closely aligned to their conversation about sounds. Hylas presents a theory of double existence where colour in itself is the motion and configuration of particles of matter in a fluid medium, and colour as sensed by us is that which in our experience we designate by colour words. Philonous then points out that it is contrary to common sense to say that colour (as opposed to the cause of colour) is really a kind of motion that is not seen at all but possibly felt by touch. Hylas does not have any further rebuttal to the mind-dependence of colour and so the discussion moves on to a different topic.

NOTES

1 As can be seen, for example, in Keith Allen's *A Naïve Realist Theory of Colour* (2016).
2 For a comprehensive study of theories of light with focus on Britain and Ireland see Cantor (1983).

FURTHER READING

For a critical examination of Berkeley's argumentative strategy in the first dialogue See Georges Dicker, *Berkeley's Idealism: A Critical Examination* (Oxford University Press 2011), chapter 5. For a defence of Berkeley's approach see Sam Rickless, *Berkeley's*

Argument for Idealism (Oxford University Press 2013), chapter 4. For a hands-on, experimental approach to Berkeley's claims about sensation see David Berman, *A Manual of Experimental Philosophy* (Jeremy Pepyat Books 2009).

Margaret Wilson (1987), "Berkeley on the mind-dependence of colors", *Pacific Philosophical Quarterly*, 68: 249–64, is a helpful and largely sympathetic paper on Berkeley's discussion of colour. Lisa Downing, "Sensible qualities and secondary qualities in the first dialogue", in Stefan Storrie (ed.), *Berkeley's Three Dialogues: New Essays* (Oxford University Press 2018) adds to Wilson's picture.

4

THE NATURE OF THE SENSIBLE II

I wonder how men cannot see a truth so obvious, as that extension
cannot exist without a thinking substance.

Notebooks §270

THE PRIMARY–SECONDARY QUALITY DISTINCTION

We could imagine that at this point of the dialogue Hylas is in a
mild panic because he has been forced into the sceptical position he
abhors about a number of sensible qualities. Fortunately, he recalls
a distinction within the class of sensible qualities that "several philosophers maintain" (187). This is the distinction between 'primary'
and 'secondary' qualities. Included among the former are extension,
figure, solidity, gravity, motion and rest (187), whereas the latter
are constituted by the sensible qualities discussed so far throughout
the dialogue (187–8).

The classic expression of this distinction is found in Locke's
Essay. In his terminology, a 'quality' is the power of an object to
produce an idea in our minds. Primary qualities, such as solidity,

extension, figure and mobility, are completely inseparable from objects and can be found in every particle of matter. Secondary qualities are not a second set of qualities that objects have, but the powers those things possess in virtue of their primary qualities to produce in us sensations such as colours, sounds and tastes. In Locke's words:

> What I have said concerning *Colours* and *Smells*, may be understood also of *Tastes* and *Sounds, and other the like sensible Qualities*; which, whatever reality we, by mistake, attribute to them, are in truth nothing in the Objects themselves, but Powers to produce various Sensations in us, and *depend on those primary Qualities, viz.* Bulk, Figure, Texture, and Motion of parts; as I have said.
>
> (*Essay* 2.8.14)

Presented in this light, the primary–secondary quality distinction is based on a theory of the structure of physical objects and their interaction with the human sensory system. This theory is known as 'corpuscularianism', advanced most prominently by René Descartes and Pierre Gassendi and further developed by Robert Boyle in his works *Sceptical Chymist* (1661) and *The Origin of Forms and Qualities* (1666) into a system accepted by most British and Irish scientists at the time of the publication of the *Three Dialogues*. On this view, physical objects are made out of small (though in contrast with atomism, not in theory indivisible) particles called 'corpuscles'. These particles have one set of properties, size, figure, and so on, which are in the objects themselves and as such they have the power to bring about ideas of those qualities in our minds. Qualities that we typically attribute to objects such as colours and smells are not likewise brought about in us by those colours and smells really existing in the objects, but are, rather, caused by the primary qualities through their interactions with us. For example, the texture of an object causes it to reflect light in a certain way, that light may then enter the eye of a perceiver and send signals to a person's brain that produce, in her, the awareness of the colour green. It is, then, this object's particular texture that has the power to, at least in part, determine how we perceive the colour of the object. Here is one of Locke's examples:

Pound an Almond, and the clear white *Colour* will be altered into a dirty one, and the sweet *Taste* into an oily one. What real Alteration can the beating of the Pestle make in any Body, but an Alteration of the *Texture* of it?

(*Essay* 2.8.20)

Locke's theory suggests that the ideas of primary qualities have more than a merely contingent connection to our ideas. Our idea of an object's shape depends on the actual shape of the object. In fact, Locke states that this relation is one of resemblance:

the *Ideas of primary Qualities* of Bodies, *are Resemblances* of them, and their Patterns do really exist in the Bodies themselves; But the *Ideas, produced* in us *by* these *Secondary Qualities, have no resemblance* of them at all.

(*Essay* 2.8.15)

There has been a significant amount of debate among Locke scholars about whether Locke really believed that ideas or primary qualities resembled the primary qualities in objects. I am following Michael Jacovides (1999) in thinking that this resemblance is a reasonable and straightforward consequence of Locke's position. After all, Locke's corpuscularian scientific programme is informed by our experience of how things are in the world. To some extent then, it is reasonable to think that for Locke the assignment of certain qualities as primary is dependent on our ideas of primary qualities, and that the connection between events concerning physical objects is based on our observation of our ideas of them. If there is not a resemblance between these ideas and qualities, there would seem little experiential support for corpuscularianism itself. For example, it seems reasonable that Locke believes that we can surmise from our experience that the solidity, number, extension, texture and so on, not only of the *idea of the pestle* beating the almond, but of the *actual pestle* beating the almond, are at work and are causally responsible for the change in our ideas and corresponding change in the qualities of the almond.

This theory is significant at this point in the *Three Dialogues* because it supplies a criterion for distinguishing between true and apparent sensible qualities such as shape in terms of a correspondence between our idea of the shape and the shape of the object. As we saw in their discussion of colour in particular, Hylas had trouble finding a criterion for 'true' colour that appealed to the nature of a mind-independent object rather than our mere perception of the object. The primary–secondary quality distinction is consistent with the lack of such criteria but, at the same time, it offers hope that such a criterion will be present for our perception of primary qualities. In response to Hylas' distinction between primary and secondary qualities, Philonous will continue, in a rather relentless fashion, to submit the so-called primary qualities to the conflicting appearances argument. Towards the end of their discussion they will also return to examine a kind of assimilation argument. I am in agreement with a number of scholars, such as Barry Stroud (1980), Catherine Wilson (1982) and Lisa Downing (2018), that in the first dialogue Philonous' primary concern is to refute the most articulate form of materialism, namely the corpuscularian theory of primary and secondary qualities.

RELATIVITY OF EXTENSION

The central sensible quality under discussion in this part of the dialogue is 'extension'. Philonous argues that extension and figure are relative in three senses. First, these sensible qualities are relative to different kinds of perceivers (188–9). If we assume that small animals like mites perceive the world as spatially arranged in roughly the same way that humans do, then to the mite, its foot would seem quite large, about the same size as our feet look to us. A breadcrumb to a mite would look like a large rock looks to us. If sensible things are mind-independent, externally existing things that have the qualities that we immediately perceive, then the mite's foot and the breadcrumb are both large and small at the same time, but that leads to material substance possessing contradictory properties. One response to this argument, which Hylas unfortunately does not raise, would be to say that extension is measured not with reference to the different size of the bodies of different animals, but to a thing that is constant in size, such as a measuring rod. The true magnitude of the extension of the mite's foot, it might then be thought, is not much of an issue. It is simply compared for size with a second, invariable thing. But measuring extension in this way is different from sensing size. What

Philonous is interested in is how things are sensed, not how objects compare next to other objects that are used to measure length. The question is not whether the mite's foot is smaller or larger than a measuring rod, but whether the mite's foot is large or small. For the mite, the measuring rod appears very large, to a human it is not large at all. Again, who is right? The case here is analogous to the criterion of true colour in case of normal human perception in sunlight. It is a fine criterion, but it does not get at a mind-independent, objective feature of the object as it is in itself, but chooses an arbitrary criterion in order to allow for agreement between people over time.

Second, things appear smaller and larger, and have different shapes, depending on our perceptual situation at different times. For example, if I look at a house close up, it might look large and square, but from further away it will look small and round (189). Thirdly, things can look different to the same person at the same time, just as in the bucket of water example. If I look at an object with one eye bare and the other eye looking through a microscope, the object I am looking at will "to one eye [. . .] seem little, smooth, and round, when at the same time it appears to the other, great, uneven, and angular" (189).

Philonous presents analogous arguments with regard also to motion and solidity. We will not cover these arguments here for while they are interesting in their own right they are brief and add little to the overall picture of Berkeley's procedure in the dialogue. However, Philonous' next point is interesting as it shows something about how Berkeley sees his materialist targets. Philonous states that:

> if extension be once acknowledged to have no existence without the mind, the same must necessarily be granted of motion, solidity, and gravity, since they all evidently suppose extension. It is therefore superfluous to inquire particularly concerning each of them. In denying extension, you have denied them all to have any real existence.
>
> (191)

The idea here is that extension is the fundamental property of matter that makes all other primary qualities possible. Extension is seen as a, as it were, 'super-primary' quality. This is a position that is famously held by Descartes who stated that everything "which can be attributed to body presupposes extension, and is merely a mode of an extended thing" (*Principles* AT VIIIA 25; CSM I 210). Locke, however, did not hold this view. The difference between them on this matter stems from the different assumption about the structure of the physical world that different forms of corpuscularianism endorsed. Descartes was a 'plenist'. He thought space was a plenum, that matter takes up every region of space and fills each part of every region, no matter how small, so there was no empty space anywhere. This requires matter to be infinitely divisible in order to take up every possible part of space. It follows that all other primary qualities, such as figure and solidity, which depend on matter's having parts, can always be divided further. The only property that persists through such an infinite division is the purely mathematical concept of pure extension, and, for this reason, that property is seen as fundamental. Locke, on the other hand, was an 'atomist' and held that matter was not infinitely divisible, but consists of minute shaped particles that can collide and transfer motion to each other. Therefore, he holds that there are three fundamental properties that belong to matter, extension, solidity and the capacity to transfer motion. (*Essay* 2.23.17). We saw above that the primary qualities that Philonous submits to the conflicting appearances argument are precisely those that are most fundamental to Locke: extension, solidity and motion. In this way Philonous is signalling that he is arguing against both the Cartesian plenist and the Lockean atomist versions of corpuscularianism.

The discussion about the relativity of primary qualities has so far only addressed what I have called the 'metaphysical' application of the argument, which shows that material substance has conflicting properties such as large and small at the same time. This was a point made already by Bayle:

> Add to this, that all the ways of suspension which destroy the reality of corporeal qualities, overthrows the reality of extension. Since the same bodies are sweet to some men, and bitter to others, it may reasonably be inferred that they are neither sweet nor bitter in their own nature, and absolutely speaking. [. . .] Why should we not say the same thing of extension?
>
> (Bayle 1734–8: 5.612, "Zeno of Elea")

While the argument initially overwhelms Hylas, we have seen that he has the resources to resist the conclusion that his conception of material substance is contradictory. In the *Principles*, Berkeley himself commented on the kind of argument Philonous and Bayle put against the materialist:

> In short, let any one consider those arguments, which are thought manifestly to prove that colours and tastes exist only in the mind, and he shall find they may with equal force, be brought to prove the same thing of extension, figure, and motion. Though it must be confessed this method of arguing doth not so much prove that there is no extension or colour in an outward object, as that we do not know by sense which is the true extension or colour of the object.
>
> (*Principles* 15)

Can we know by sense what the true and the merely apparent extension of a mind-independent object is? We saw with the secondary qualities that Hylas will often at this point aim to distinguish between true and apparent sensible qualities to avoid the contradiction. This manifests in two different ways.

One approach, which Hylas also tried in the case of colour, is to distinguish true from apparent colour in terms of a privileged perceptual situation that identifies which visual experience is the experience of the true colour. Could he attempt this in the case of extension? This approach might have promise. After all, if our idea of, for example, shape resembles the shape in the object itself, then, it would seem that the true shape could be sufficiently similar to the actual shape to allow for this. Consider, for example, Locke's claim that "A Circle or Square are the same, whether in *Idea* or Existence" (*Essay* 2.8.18). But this is where the conflicting appearances argument is at its most forceful. The problem with resemblance is that our knowledge of this resemblance goes from our ideas out to the object in itself. Hylas has accepted that our ideas of extension are exceedingly variable. In order to find a privileged perceptual standpoint within our ideas of extension that is not merely stipulative but which indicates a resemblance to the extension in the object itself, we would need a conception of the extension of the object itself. But it is precisely the lack of such a conception that has led us to look for the criterion within our ideas in the first place and therefore this procedure seems problematically circular. If we cannot determine, for example, what the true extension of an object is, then we have no way of understanding or modelling the causal connection between its perceived extension and its real extension. This represents a challenge to the materialist corpuscularian contention and forces its adherents to offer a scientific explanation of how primary qualities give rise to ideas, of any kind, in our minds. If this approach is successful, then it can show that the corpuscularian materialist theory cannot explain what it purports to explain, but not that the materialistic assumption that underlies the theory is false.

ON ABSTRACTION

Hylas' other approach is to argue that true and apparent sensible qualities are radically distinct objects of different sense modalities. Typically, the true sensible quality is really a kind of motion and the merely apparent sound or colour is an idea of a secondary quality. It might seem that this option is not really open to him now. Once we start to look for a stable and objective criterion for true extension in some more basic and objective quality we get into trouble. Because extension is supposed to be the most fundamental of the sensible qualities, there does not seem to be any further more basic and purportedly objective level of explanation to appeal to. The primary qualities are supposed to do explanatory work. This is obviously the case for the 'plenist' version of materialism, but probably also for the 'atomist' version according to which extension is at the most basic level of primary qualities together with solidity and motion. Nevertheless, this is the route that Hylas in fact takes. He believes this might work because the criterion he will appeal to is not strictly a sensible quality but an idea from which the mind has abstracted away the uncertain and changing relational qualities that made sensible qualities poor candidates to establish the criterion of true perceptions.

> *H:* It is just come into my head, Philonous, that I have somewhere heard of a distinction between absolute and sensible extension. Now though it be acknowledged that great and small, consisting merely in the relation which other extended beings have to the parts of our own bodies, do not really inhere in the substances themselves; yet nothing obliges us to hold the same with regard to absolute extension, which is something

> abstracted from great and small, from this or that particular
> magnitude or figure. So likewise as to motion, swift and slow
> are altogether relative to the succession of ideas in our own
> minds. But it does not follow, because those modifications
> of motion exist not without the mind, that therefore absolute
> motion abstracted from them does not. (192)

Hylas now concedes that sensible qualities of large and small are
not in objects, but are mere relations between our body and external objects. He then suggests that there is a kind of non-relational
extension, in other words 'absolute extension'. This is a notion of
extension according to which all sensible and relational qualities,
such as particular sizes and particular shapes, have been separated
out, leaving the bare notion of extension. Hylas does not specify how
this notion of extension would function as a stable, objective quality
in external objects to which we can hold up and compare the changing mind-dependent ideas. What is considered is rather the possibility
that there is such a thing as absolute extension, regardless of its function. Philonous then begins to question this conception of extension:

> P: Pray what is it that distinguishes one motion, or one part of
>   extension, from another? Is it not something sensible, as some
>   degree of swiftness or slowness, some certain magnitude or
>   figure peculiar to each?
> H: I think so.
> P: These qualities, therefore, stripped of all sensible proper-
>   ties, are without all specific and numerical differences, as the
>   Schools call them.
> H: They are.
> P: That is to say, they are extension in general, and motion in
>   general.
> H: Let it be so.
> P: But it is a universally received maxim, that 'everything which
>   exists, is particular'. How then can motion in general, or exten-
>   sion in general, exist in any corporeal substance? (192–3)

Philonous first states that as the abstract notion of extension that
Hylas is proposing exists in each external object, abstract extension

in external objects does not have any feature that distinguishes it from any other instance. From this he concludes that it is extension in general. Absolute extension is then a rather odd entity. It must exist in each extended object in the same way. This amounts to the view that the same, numerically identical thing exists in many things. This, he argues, is problematic because it is typically believed that everything that exists is particular. Every instance of the quality of extension is unique and not something shared by each instance, as absolute extension would be shared by each extended thing. To say that everything that exists is particular is a "universally received maxim" is a bit too strong. In metaphysics this claim could be recognized as a form of nominalism, but far from everyone is committed to nominalism. For example, on some interpretations of Plato's forms, they are general in this sense. Nevertheless, Locke felt he could simply state without argument that "All things, that exist, [are] particulars" (*Essay* 3.3.1). Philonous is, then, pointing out that by positing absolute extension Hylas is in conflict with a basic metaphysical assumption in Locke's philosophy.

In response to this Hylas says that he "will take time to solve your difficulty" (193). But he is not given time to do so, being rather rudely interrupted by Philonous who continues his questioning in a somewhat different direction. Since Philonous does not allow Hylas to develop a defence of abstraction, it will be instructive here to take a moment to see what such a defence might look like. In Locke's *Essay* he argues that the fact that we communicate through language shows that we must be able to form abstract and general ideas. Locke introduced the notion of an abstract idea to explain how words can be general in their signification. On this view a word is only meaningful if it signifies an idea (*Essay* 3.2.2). As the number of ideas is endless, communication is only manageable if most words signify kinds of things (*Essay* 2.11.9). Given Locke's semantic constraint there must be ideas of such general things. But as nothing exists in nature or reality that is not itself particular (*Essay* 3.3.1), these ideas cannot be found in the external world, but must be generated by an inner, mental process (*Essay* 2.11.9). Locke's view is, then, not that there are abstract and general properties in objects in themselves, but that our minds can create ideas of such things. This directly avoids the conflict with nominalism. In fact, Locke's view shares many features with Aristotle, who said "the mind when it is thinking of objects of Mathematics, thinks as separate, elements which do not exist separately" (*De Anima*, 3.8, 431b15). In this way they both held a view of abstraction that tries to steer a middle ground between Platonic realism and nominalism. We might then think that such ideas could serve as a basis for a criterion of truth in the face of the relativity of our ideas of particular extensions.

Berkeley devotes the main part of the substantial Introduction to the *Principles* to combat this view. One of his central arguments, which has been analysed in some detail by Weinberg (1965) and Winkler (1989), is known as the 'argument from impossibility'. It has the following structure:

1. Everything that exists in 'nature or reality' is particular.
2. An abstract general idea would be something like an abstract, general, mental object.
3. Therefore an abstract general idea could not exist in 'nature or reality'.
4. If something is impossible (cannot exist in 'nature or reality'), then it cannot be conceived.
5. Therefore, abstract general ideas cannot be conceived, i.e., we cannot have general abstract ideas.

The argument brings together three elements that make up the three main premises of the argument. First, the view that everything that exists in nature or reality is particular (*Principles,* Introduction §15). Second, the assumption about what an abstract thing is, that it would have to be a kind of general object (*Principles*, Introduction §§7–9). From this it follows that abstract general ideas cannot exist in nature or reality. The third element is a view on the nature of the relation between possibility and conceivability, which holds that if something is impossible in the sense that it cannot exist in nature or reality, then it cannot be conceived (*Principles*, Introduction §10).[1] It then follows that as abstract general ideas cannot be conceived, it is impossible to 'have' such ideas. Because ideas do not float around outside (ontologically speaking) those who have the ideas, it is impossible for there to be such ideas.

The standard response to this argument was developed by Mackie (1976) and Taylor (1978). They came to see premise 2 as the weak point in the argument. The kind of abstraction that Berkeley is targeting in the argument is thought to lead to the positing of an abstract, general, mental object because abstraction is thought to be a *separation* of a universal property from the object. To maintain the view that it is possible to conceive of Aristotelian universals, yet also in order to be sensitive to the challenge of Berkeley's argument, one could distinguish between two different views of how abstraction leads to the conception of a general property. One version of abstraction, call it 'crude Aristotelianism', assumes that one can only conceive of a general property if one is able to separate the property in thought from the object in which it inheres. Another version of abstraction, call it 'subtle Aristotelianism', holds that conceiving of a general property does not require the relevant separation in thought. Instead the requisite abstraction is done while having the object as a whole in view. This cognitive feat is thought to be possible on the strength of the phenomenon of 'selective attention'. The suggestion is that by focusing one's attention on a feature of an object, I am not thinking of this feature as separate from the object as a whole. The object is still there confronting me in experience. What has happened is merely that there has been a shift in the act of attending rather than a shift in the object conceived. It is relevant to ask, in this context, whether a feat of selective attention, of this kind, is possible.

ASSIMILATING PRIMARY AND SECONDARY QUALITIES

Returning to the main line of discussion in the *Three Dialogues*, Philonous has now applied arguments from conflicting appearances to various primary qualities. If these arguments are successful, they show that an object's real and invariable extension, shape and so on cannot be inferred from the features that are perceived. This kind of argument is aimed at blocking the materialist from formulating her own positive theory of sensible objects as material objects by pushing her in the direction of scepticism. This is not, by itself, a positive argument for Philonous' view that sensible things are mind-dependent. As we saw when the secondary qualities were discussed, Philonous used the assimilation argument to argue that some secondary qualities were in fact identical to degrees of pain and pleasure. Since the latter are mind-dependent, so too are the secondary qualities. We now find Philonous using a similar kind of argument to defend the view that primary qualities are also mind-dependent. The discussion of abstraction in the *Three Dialogues* is in fact a step in this argument.

After making the Lockean point that everything that exists is particular, Philonous challenges Hylas to form an idea of extension that does not have any sensible features, e.g., great or small, round or square. Hylas tries but fails to conceive of such a thing. Philonous' next step is to ask Hylas if he can conceive of, for example, extension, apart from all secondary qualities. In reply to this Hylas states that mathematics treats of extension and figure while disregarding, for example, the colour of the figure in a geometrical demonstration. Philonous thinks this is correct in one sense but not in another. There are at least two ways in which we could conceive of abstraction in geometrical proofs. Following Winkler (1989) I will call them the 'contemplation' sense and the 'activity' sense. The former is what Hylas has in mind. The idea is that when we go through a geometrical proof we are able to focus our attention selectively on, for example, the triangularity of the triangle, without focusing on any particular size or colour, and so on. The latter is what Philonous is ready to accept. This is an act of abstraction according to which an object, such as a figure in a diagram is put to use in such a way that a certain feature of the object is relevant for working through the proof and reaching the desired conclusion, whereas other features are not. For example, the features of having three sides enclosing a space is a relevant feature of many of the proofs in the first books of Euclid's *Elements*, whereas in many proofs the particular shape of the triangle is irrelevant to the proof. As Philonous puts it:

P: Mathematicians treat of quantity, without regarding what other sensible qualities it is attended with, as being altogether indifferent to their demonstrations. But when laying aside the words, they contemplate the bare ideas; I believe you will find they are not the pure abstracted ideas of extension. (193)

The former view makes a claim about our cognitive abilities, that we can conceive of general features of an object through an act of selective attention whereas the latter view makes no such claim.

While selective attention is a central topic of study in current cognitive psychology and cognitive neuroscience, I am not aware of any study that has concluded, or assumed at the outset, that the product of an act of attention is a general feature of an object.

Hylas' appeal to geometrical practice does not lead him to convince Philonous that it is possible to conceive of primary qualities apart from their secondary qualities. Philonous instead asks Hylas whether he himself can form such an idea:

> P: But for your farther satisfaction, try if you can frame the idea of any figure, abstracted from all particularities of size, or even from other sensible qualities.
>
> H: Let me think a little – I do not find that I can.
>
> P: And can you think it possible, that should really exist in nature, which implies a repugnancy in its conception?
>
> H: By no means.
>
> P: Since therefore it is impossible even for the mind to disunite the ideas of extension and motion from all other sensible qualities, does it not follow, that where the one exist, there necessarily the other exist likewise?
>
> H: It should seem so.
>
> P: Consequently the very same arguments which you admitted as conclusive against the secondary qualities are, without any farther application of force, against the primary too. Besides, if you will trust your senses, is it not plain, all sensible qualities coexist, or, to them, appear as being in the same place? Do they ever represent a motion, or figure, as being divested of all other visible and tangible qualities? (194)

Philonous' argument is unfortunately very condensed but has the following steps. First, he states that primary qualities are never perceived as existing separate from secondary qualities, neither in the normal course of experience, nor through an act of abstracting and disuniting sensible qualities from other properties. We have considered the case of abstraction in some detail, but what is Hylas doing when he is trying, and failing, to conceive of extension without any secondary qualities? In a similar passage in §10 of the *Principles* Berkeley speaks of his own efforts in this regard: "For my own part, I see evidently that it is not in my power to frame an idea of a body extended and moved, but I must withal give it some colour or other sensible quality which is acknowledged to exist only in the mind." For example, if I try and conceive of the extension of a line I have drawn on a piece of paper while taking the line to have no colour, it is hard to see how I am conceiving of anything at all. It could be objected that vison is not necessary for conceiving of extension. A blind person can understand what big and small, circular and rectangular, and so on, mean. Berkeley would most certainly accept this point, but he would also hold that the blind person's conception of extension was assimilated with mind-dependent sensation. As we saw in Chapter 1, Berkeley argued in the *New Theory* that all perception of extension has tactile sensations as signifiers. I could manage this feat by tracing the mark left on the paper where I pressed down the pen. In that case I am annexing other sensations to the extension, however, this time of a tactile variety.

The second premise in Philonous' argument is that if something cannot possibly be conceived, it cannot exist in nature. We might object that Philonous has not shown that it is impossible to conceive of extension apart from any secondary quality, only that Hylas was not able to do so when put on the spot. In the end I suspect that the plausibility of Philonous' premise here depends on how successful he has been in arguing against various forms of abstraction. As we saw above Berkeley has much more to say about this in the *Principles* than he does in the *Three Dialogues*, which is unfortunate, for as Rickless (2013) has noted, his argument for the mind-dependence of primary qualities in the *Three Dialogues* depends on how successful he is in his anti-abstractionist stance. Nevertheless, from these two premises Philonous concludes that primary qualities cannot exist apart from secondary qualities. He then claims that if something is in the mind and another thing cannot exist apart from it, then that other thing must also be in the mind. Since he has argued at great length that secondary qualities are mind-dependent, as the assimilation arguments have shown, so must the primary qualities be.

THE 'MASTER ARGUMENT'

At this point in the discussion Hylas is accepting that any particular sensible quality they have considered has been shown to be mind dependent. But, he now suggests that perhaps several qualities "united or blended together" (199) depend on material substance? In response to this Philonous presents a rhetorically weighty reply that has been known as Berkeley's 'master argument' since Gallois (1974). Philonous presents a challenge to Hylas: "If you can conceive it possible for any mixture or combinations of qualities, or any sensible object whatever, to exist without the mind, then I will grant it actually to be so" (200). Philonous is raising the stakes in two ways here. First, he allows that the *possibility* of conceiving of a mind-independent sensible object (or non-object-like mixture or combination of sensible qualities) is sufficient for granting the *actuality* of that mind-independence. This is rather generous, because we typically think that not everything that is possible is actual. Second, Philonous is happy to end the discussion here and now. If Hylas can show that it is possible to conceive of a sensible thing existing independently of the mind, then Philonous will declare his immaterialism is defeated.

At the same time, it is hyperbolic to call this a 'master argument'. Philonous is not presenting a positive argument for idealism. He is not arguing: because what is conceived is in the mind, it follows that what is conceived would not exist if it were not thought of. If he did so it would not be very convincing. I might be convinced that it is impossible to conceive of my bicycle existing without a notion of my bicycle being present to my mind. But I would surely not conclude that the bicycle does not exist when I am not conceiving of it. Rather, the argument is blocking a path to the belief in material substance, namely: it is possible to conceive of a sensible thing which is not conceived of by any mind, therefore, there exist sensible things that do not depend for their existence on a mind.

Hylas is asked to conceive of the possibility of a sensible thing existing without the mind. He accepts the challenge with relish:

> H: If it comes to that, the point will soon be decided. What more easy than to conceive a tree or house existing by itself, independent of, and unperceived by, any mind whatsoever? I do at this present time conceive them existing after that manner. (200)

Hylas' approach to the challenge is to imagine a tree and supposing that it is not perceived by anyone, there are no people or birds or insects etc. there to perceive it. Hylas has to imagine the sensible object rather than sensing it, because if he sensed it, he believes that it would most certainly be in his mind. Philonous is happy to accept this approach because imagination and sensation both have as their object sensible qualities, though the former are typically fainter and less connected with the sensible world as a whole.

The discussion continues as follows:

> *P:* How say you, Hylas, can you see a thing which is at the same time unseen?
>
> *H:* No, that were a contradiction.
>
> *P:* Is it not as great a contradiction to talk of 'conceiving' a thing which is 'unconceived'?
>
> *H:* It is.
>
> *P:* The tree or house therefore, which you think of, is conceived by you.
>
> *H:* How should it be otherwise?
>
> *P:* And what is conceived is surely in the mind?
>
> *H:* Without question, that which is conceived is in the mind.
>
> *P:* How then came you to say, you conceived a house or tree existing independent and out of all minds whatsoever?
>
> *H:* That was I own an oversight. (200)

Philonous objects to Hylas' approach because in imagining the tree, the tree is conceived by Hylas' and therefore exists in Hylas' mind. In trying to conceive of a thing that is unconceived in this way, Hylas attempts something contradictory because the very act of conceiving runs contrary to what he aims to achieve, that the thing he conceives of is unconceived. This is how Hylas diagnoses his attempt:

> *H:* As I was thinking of a tree in a solitary place, where no one was present to see it, methought that was to conceive a tree as existing unperceived or unthought of, not considering that I myself conceived it all the while. But now I plainly see that all I can do is to frame ideas in my own mind. I may indeed conceive in my own thoughts the idea of a tree, or a house, or a mountain, but that is all. And this is far from proving that I can conceive them 'existing out of the minds of all spirits'. (200)

But we might think that Hylas gives up much too quickly. We might for example think he should emphasize a distinction between what is 'in our mind' when we conceive of the tree and the tree out in the real world that we are thinking of by means of that idea. If we do so, we can say that the idea is conceived by us, whereas the tree itself exists unconceived. Hylas might not accept that to represent an object by means of an idea amounts to conceiving of the tree itself as a sensible thing. What is conceived as a sensible thing is the idea, with all its sensible qualities. When asked to describe what the thing represented is like, as a sensible object, he would presumably say that it has just the same properties as the ideas in his mind. It then seems difficult to see how Hylas can uphold the distinction between idea and representation. To get clear on these issues it will be instructive to consider the wider discussion about theories of perception in which the discussion of the so-called 'master argument' is sandwiched.

THEORIES OF PERCEPTION

In the discussion of direct and indirect perception at the outset of the first dialogue Philonous and Hylas both agreed on a simple theory of perception: that what is immediately sensed is the sensible object or a part thereof. This has been an important component in the discussion that, together with Hylas' materialist commitment, has allowed Philonous to lead Hylas down the road to scepticism. So far, Hylas has been trying to avoid such conclusions by challenging Philonous on the nature of the sensible. He has done so by distinguishing aspects of what is sensed and aiming to establish distinctions between kinds of sensible qualities, be it the doctrine of double existence, the primary/secondary quality distinction, or the distinction between, on the one hand, the abstract and general, and on the other hand, the concrete and particular.

This approach has not been successful for Hylas, so at this point in the dialogue he reconsiders the theory of sense perception that has been assumed from the outset. As he now says to Philonous: "One great oversight I take to be this: that I did not sufficiently distinguish the object from the sensation. Now though this later may not exist without the mind, yet it will not thence follow that the former cannot" (194). The line he now wants to pursue is to consider theories of perception that allow that the sensation and the object that is sensed are distinct. The initial theory understood perception only in terms of perceivers and the things sensed, i.e., the sensible qualities. The new theories, because they distinguish the sensation from the sensible object perceived, must consist of at least three components, the perceiver, the sensation and the sensible object. The two theories that Hylas considers are commonly known as the 'act–object' theory and the 'representational' theory. The act–object theory holds that the sensation is not an object but a certain kind of act in the subject. Such an analysis of perception does not posit the sensation as a third thing (understood as an object) between the object and the perceiver, but instead, just as the simple theory assumed at the outset, takes the perceiver, through the act of sensation, to be in direct contact with sensible objects. This sort of theory is, therefore, classified as a direct realist theory of perception. Nevertheless, by placing the sensation in the mind of the perceiver, where the original theory identified the sensation with the object, it does distinguish between the sensation and the object, in accordance with Hylas' promises. The representational theory holds that we know sensible objects through an intermediary object, the sensation, which functions as a representation of the object. Accordingly, this theory falls within the category of indirect realism.

In the early modern period we find the contrast between, and articulation of, these two theories of perception, in the famous and heated debate between the two French theologians and Cartesian philosophers Malebranche and Antoine Arnauld. The dispute started with the publication of Arnauld's *On True and False Ideas* (1683) which was a response to Malebranche's *Treatise on Nature and Grace* (1680) but also against the general articulation of Malebranche's Cartesianism in the *Search*. The dispute, which ranged over a number of philosophical and theological issues and involved many of the leading intellectuals at the time, continued into the 1700s.

In his 1683 work, Arnauld argues against Malebranche's theory of knowledge summarized by the claim that we see all things in God. The dispute centred on the correct way to understand Descartes' conception of 'idea'. In the third meditation Descartes states that ideas can be understood in two different ways. On the one hand, they may be understood as having the same nature on account of their originating in the subject, as being 'perceptions'. On the other hand, they may be understood as pointing towards things of a different nature outside the subject, as 'ideas' of various things. For Arnauld, the conception of idea as perception took precedence. The perception is identified with a change in the perceiver's mind, not with the production of an intermediary entity that in some way connects both to my mind and to the external object. To use the vocabulary of the *Three Dialogues*, he places the sensation in the mind of the perceiver. Malebranche, on the other hand, thought that an intermediary (which he located in God's mind, hence we see all things in God) is necessary because the perception by itself is not sufficient to represent the object. This is because the objects that I think about are in many cases of an utterly different nature from my mind and the changes my mind undergoes in perception. Malebranche argued that I can think of objects, such a geo-metrical objects, which include the notions of necessity, eternity and universality, but there is nothing like that in my perceptions.

While Arnauld's position would be the most well-known presenta-tion of an act–object theory at the time, it would also be anachronistic to simply equate Hylas with Arnauld here. One reason for this is that the discussion between Hylas and Philonous in the first dialogue is strictly concerned with sense perception, whereas Arnauld's theory aims to be a general theory of perception that covers also the per-ception of mathematical, scientific and theological concepts. The act–object theory is presented in the following way:

P: Make me understand the difference between what is immedi-ately perceived and a sensation.

H: The sensation I take to be an act of the mind perceiving; beside which there is something perceived, and this I call the object. For example, there is red and yellow on that tulip. But then the act of perceiving those colours is in me only, and not in the tulip.

P: What tulip do you speak of? Is it that which you see?

H: The same.

P: And what do you see beside colour, figure, and extension?

H: Nothing.

P: What you would say then is that the red and yellow are coexistent with the extension; is it not?

H: That is not all; I would say that they have a real existence with-out the mind, in some unthinking substance. (195–6)

In a way Hylas is starting from the beginning again. He is reneging on the primary–secondary quality distinction and instead seemingly arguing that all sensible qualities, such as the red and yellow colour, as well as extension, are in the mind-independent object, in this case, the tulip. On this view the sensation is an act of the mind perceiving, such as the act of perceiving the red and yellow on the tulip, and what is immediately perceived is the sensible object, the tulip which is red and yellow. This is a direct realist view because there is no intermediary object between the perceiver and the mind-independent sensible object, rather, the mind-dependent sensation is the (mind-dependent) act of directly perceiving the (mind-independent) sensible object.

Philonous' argument against this view has two main components. First, he argues that the act–object view will lead to an absurdity if perception is not an act. Second, he argues that for perception to be an act is for the perception to be an act of will. But no act of will is in fact involved in sense perception. The conclusion is that the act–object view either must accept that perception is not an act in which case the theory leads to an absurdity, or it must accept that the act is an act of will, which is a conclusion that is not commensurate with the fact of perception. The first component of this reply is presented in the following way:

P: To return then to your distinction between 'sensation' and 'object'; if I take you right, you distinguish in every perception two things, the one an action of the mind, the other not.

H: True.

P: And this action cannot exist in, or belong to, any unthinking thing; but whatever beside is implied in a perception, may.

H: That is my meaning.

P: So that if there was a perception without any act of the mind, it were possible such a perception should exist in an unthinking substance.

H: I grant it. But it is impossible there should be such a perception. (196)

Philonous' argument is that according to the act–object view the sensation is an act that cannot exist in an unthinking thing, but whatever is not an act but somehow belongs to the perception, that is, what the sensation represents, points to, or implies, can exist in a mind-independent being. Mind-dependence and activity are tied together on this view, such that if there were a sensation that did not evidence activity, it could exist in a mind-independent thing. A situation in which a mind-independent thing could perceive is seen as absurd by both Hylas and Philonous, for it would mean that things without consciousness could perceive colours, or most absurdly, pain and pleasure. Hylas agrees on this conditional statement but assures Philonous that activity is always included in sense perception.

So far Philonous has drawn out the implications of the act–object theory. In the second component they examine the 'what it is like'-ness of sense perception without such theoretical assumptions and conclude that sense perception is in fact entirely passive. When this finding is combined with the theoretical assumptions of the act–object theory, the conclusion is that the theory leads to the absurdity of the possibility of unthinking things that perceive. The second component has two parts, the first is as follows:

P: When is the mind said to be active?
H: When it produces, puts an end to, or changes anything.
P: Can the mind produce, discontinue, or change anything but by an act of the will?
H: It cannot.
P: The mind therefore is to be accounted active in its perceptions, so far forth as volition is included in them.
H: It is.

In the first part they agree on a conception of activity in perception. For the mind to be active is for it to "produce, discontinue, or change" something. For the mind to do this it must exert an act of will. This crucial part of the argument might seem rather weak. It seems open to Hylas to say that some mental activity is not best characterised as an act of will, but in a weaker sense of the mind undergoing some change. For example, Arnauld, following a long tradition of scholastic thinkers, holds a weaker conception of mental activity than act of will: "When I say that the soul does this or that, and that it has the faculty of doing this or that, I understand by the word 'do' the perception that it has of objects, which is one of its modifications" (TFI [1990], ch. 5, p. 67). On this view mental activity could simply be an actualization of a capacity of the mental faculty, which can be either active or passive.

Jennifer Marušić (2018) has suggested that our two protagonists have agreed that mental activity must be an act of will on the basis of their agreed conception of sensible qualities earlier in the dialogue. Specifically, that they have agreed to take sensible qualities to be things that appear to us in sensation. Included in the notion of something appearing to us is the idea that it has an introspectible phenomenal character, in other words, that there is something that it is like for it to appear. If this is granted it is a short step to conclude that an appearance is something with respect to which we are passive, it is something that happens to us, not something that we do. Hylas has distinguished between the act, which he calls the sensation, and the sensible quality. The former is on the side of the subject and the latter is in the object of perception. The idea behind Hylas' theory is to distinguish the act or sensation from the sensible quality. As the sensible quality is an appearance and appearances have phenomenal character and are things that happen to us, the mental act would supposedly have to have at least one feature that is different from the sensible quality. It is unlikely that Hylas would want to deny that the mental act has some content of which we can be introspectively aware, as it is supposed to be the mind-dependent aspect of experience. Instead, he would have to distinguish the act from the sensible quality by maintaining that the act is something we do, an act of will, not something that merely happens to us.

In the second part of this discussion of the act–object theory Philonous presents a number of examples of sense perception in which he claims that no volition by the mind is involved.

P: In plucking a flower, I am active, because I do it by the motion of my hand, which was consequent upon my volition; so likewise in applying it to my nose. But is either of these smelling?

H: No.

P: I act too in drawing the air through my nose; because my breathing so, rather than otherwise, is the effect of my volition. But neither can this be called 'smelling'; for if it were, I should smell every time I breathed in that manner.

H: True.

P: Smelling then is somewhat consequent to all this.

H: It is.

P: But I do not find my will concerned any farther. Whatever more there is, as that I perceive such a particular smell or any smell at all, this is independent of my will, and therein I am altogether passive. Do you find it otherwise with you, Hylas?

H: No, the very same.

P: Then as to seeing, is it not in your power to open your eyes, or keep them shut; to turn them this or that way?

H: Without doubt.

P: But does it in like manner depend on your will that, in looking on this flower, you perceive white rather than any other colour? Or directing your open eyes toward yonder part of the heaven, can you avoid seeing the sun? Or is light or darkness the effect of your volition?

H: No, certainly.

P: You are then in these respects altogether passive.

H: I am.

P: Tell me now, whether seeing consists in perceiving light and colours, or in opening and turning the eyes?

H: Without doubt, in the former.

P: Since therefore you are in the very perception of light and colours altogether passive, what is become of that action you were speaking of as an ingredient in every sensation? (197)

Philonous' point here is that whereas a number of acts may precede a perception, such as plucking a flower, drawing in air through the nose, opening one's eyes, and so on, none of these acts are involved in the very sensation itself, such as the perception of scent and colour. We have control over whether we will receive sensations or not to some extent, but once we are in a position to sense, the sensations arise in us entirely involuntary. He then reminds Hylas about what they have agreed on in the first component:

P: And does it not follow from your own concessions that the perception of light and colours, including no action in it, may exist in an unperceiving substance? And is not this a plain contradiction?

H: I know not what to think of it. (197)

Why do Hylas and Philonous think that such a strange conclusion follows from their discussion of the act–object theory? Hylas' act–object model has two features, the sensation and the sensible quality. The sensation is an act, which cannot exist in an unthinking thing but must exist in the mind of a perceiver, but whatever is not an act but somehow belongs to the perception, namely the sensible quality, is mind-independent and so exists in a mind-independent being. Since Hylas has been made to accept that there is no act corresponding to the sensation, what he is left with, if he still holds on to his general model, is a sensible quality, which is both a perception and something that exists independently of mind. In other words, it is a mind-independent sense experience located in the object.

If the conclusion that the character of perceptual experience is entirely exhausted by what appears in experience, so that a distinction between act and object is impossible to maintain, what does this say about Philonous' (and therefore also Berkeley's) theory of perception? Some scholars take the lesson from this exchange to be that Berkeley holds that there are no perceptual objects, only perceptual acts (Pitcher 1969; Frankel 2013). This is referred to as an 'adverbial' theory of perception, which holds that sensations are ways of sensing rather than objects sensed. For example, having the sensation of, for example, blue, is to 'sense bluely'. However, this view has a number of problems as Winkler (1989: 290ff) and Marušić (2018: 51ff) have pointed out. First, as we have seen, the conclusion reached by Hylas and Philonous is that as sensations are appearances, sensations are objects, not acts. Second, if sensations are acts, then features such as 'blue' belong to the act. As these acts are acts of mind, these features belong to the mind, so that the mind or its acts are blue, square, etc. when perceiving blueness, squareness, etc. Berkeley, reasonably, denies that this is the case (PHK 49).

If the collapse of the distinction between act and object does not favour the reduction into act, how does the reduction of the distinction into object fare? Such accounts have been put forward by Stoneham (2002: 54ff) and Marušić (2018: 52ff). Stoneham's theory, which he calls the 'Simplest Model of Perception' (SMP) is a rather austere relational theory of perception in which perception is an irreducible relation between a subject and an object that does not involve any kind of mental state in the perceiver at all. Thus, when I look at one object and then at another, I, as subject, do not directly undergo any change, rather the change is analysed in terms of a change in the relation between a subject and object. Marušić similarly accepts that mental acts do not have any role to play in Berkeley's theory of perception. Unlike the SMP, however, her view is that perception is not in the first place determined by a subject–object *relation*, but by the kind of *object* perceived. She fittingly calls this the 'object-first' model of perception. On this view sensible things are a kind of object such that the mere experience of one is sufficient for perception to occur. A thorough assessment of these proposals cannot be undertaken here. My view is that Marušić is gesturing towards something that seems important to Berkeley. After all, the entire *Three Dialogues* up to this point has been an attempt to gain understanding into what sensible things, as objects of perception, are. There can be little doubt that the character of this kind of object is pertinent to his conception of perception.

At the same time, we should be cautious in reading too much into Berkeley's, or even Philonous', theory of perception on the basis of the passage under discussion. Much of what is said is based on Hylas' deep-seated materialist assumptions of sensations as modes or properties of mind-independent substances. Further, the two 'anti-act' views' strong commitment to the passivity of the subject of perception are hard to square with what Berkeley says elsewhere. As we saw in the discussion of the *New Theory* in Chapter 1, Berkeley thinks that complex learning processes in the subject are required for perception of the three dimensional outer world. Further, as we will see in Chapter 7, Berkeley also thinks that the very notion of objectivity and of unity requires activity in thought by the subject. These are features of perception emphasized by those sympathetic to a broadly 'constructivist' or 'Kantian' reading of Berkeley's theory of perception (Hill 2018; Storrie 2012). It is a not inconsiderable challenge to present a perceptual theory for Berkeley that can take all of these features into account.

Returning to the dialectic of the *Three Dialogues*, while Hylas does not find any reply to the problems Philonous raises for the act–object theory, he makes another attempt to ground his materialism on an alternative theory of perception. Towards the end of the dialogue the discussion turns to indirect realism.

H: To speak the truth, Philonous, I think there are two kinds of objects, the one perceived immediately, which are likewise called 'ideas'; the other are real things or external objects perceived by the mediation of ideas, which are their images and representations. Now I own, ideas do not exist without the mind; but the latter sort of objects do. I am sorry I did not think of this distinction sooner; it would probably have cut short your discourse. (203)

As we have seen previously in the dialogue, Hylas has assumed indirect realism at several points in the discussion of individual sensible qualities. A kind of indirect realism underlies both the doctrine of double existence and the distinction between primary and secondary ideas. However, as Hylas had already agreed with Philonous on the simple, direct alternative theory of perception he found his position to be internally inconsistent at every turn. Now the indirect perceptual theory itself is up for discussion.

With the discussion of the act–object theory we saw that Hylas introduced an act between the subject and object of perception, but as the act was just what the subject does when it perceives, it is not an intermediary entity between the subject and object of perception. Here Hylas does introduce an intermediary entity, the idea that is separate from the real, external sensible things. Because of this, he must also reject one of the basic premises that has grounded their discussion so far, the view that sensible things are immediately perceived by sense. Philonous is incredulous when he hears this, but Hylas tries to convince him as follows:

H: For example, when I look on a picture or statue of Julius Caesar, I may be said after a manner to perceive him (though not immediately) by my senses.

P: It seems then, you will have our ideas, which alone are immediately perceived, to be pictures of external things; and that these also are perceived by sense, inasmuch as they have a conformity or resemblance to our ideas.

H: That is my meaning.

P: And in the same way that Julius Caesar, in himself invisible, is nevertheless perceived by sight, real things, in themselves imperceptible, are perceived by sense.

H: In the very same. (203)

Hylas' idea here is to model his view of perception on the way things like statues or photographs represent people or objects. His claim is that things like statues represent the people they are statues of, by being likenesses of those people. Further, this likeness is seen by means of directly perceiving the statue. The sensible thing that I directly perceive is the gateway that allows me to access the non-present object. Philonous replies by arguing that more than mere sense perception is involved in perceiving the thing represented by what is immediately perceived.

> *P:* Tell me, Hylas, when you behold the picture of Julius Caesar, do you see with your eyes any more than some colours and figures, with a certain symmetry and composition of the whole?
>
> *H:* Nothing else.
>
> *P:* And would not a man, who had never known anything of Julius Caesar, see as much?
>
> *H:* He would.
>
> *P:* Consequently he has his sight, and the use of it, in as perfect a degree as you.
>
> *H:* I agree with you.
>
> *P:* Whence comes it then that your thoughts are directed to the Roman Emperor, and his are not? This cannot proceed from the sensations or ideas of sense by you then perceived, since you acknowledge you have no advantage over him in that respect. It should seem therefore to proceed from reason and memory, should it not?
>
> *H:* It should. (203–4)

Philonous presents Hylas with the case of two people looking at the same statue of Julius Caesar. One of the people knows who the Roman general was and has seen other pictures and/or statutes of him, while the other person has no idea who Caesar was. Do they perceive the same thing or not? It is probable that they would describe their sensations in different terms. The first person would say that they saw a statue of Julius Caesar, indeed that they saw a representation of him. However, the second person, not knowing who was represented by the statue, would instead describe what she saw as the statue of a man with certain features, wearing certain clothes and so on. The question is then what explains why Caesar is represented to one person and not to the other. Philonous' point is that the cause of this discrepancy is not what is sensed, because what is sensed is the same for both persons. Instead, the source of the representational function is internal, understood as either memory or reason. Hylas introduces this example because he thinks that the statue of Caesar is analogous to how sense perception allows us to see sensible, mind-independent things. Philonous' point is, then, that on Hylas' proposed representational model of perception, the object, whatever it is, is not in fact perceived by sense, either directly or indirectly.

This concession allows Philonous to introduce a staple of Berkeley's argumentative arsenal, which is generally known as the 'likeness principle'. This principle states that a sensation or idea can only be like another sensation or idea. A non-sensible material substance cannot be like a colour or a sound or any other sensation. It seems, then, that Hylas must sever the relation between the sensation and the object sensed. This has the consequence that if what we sense, our ideas, are wholly unlike external reality, then it would seem that everything we perceive by sense is unreal.

If we recall the beginning of the dialogue, the occasion of the discussion was the challenge to present the least sceptical position with regard to sensible things. As Philonous is quick to point out, Hylas is now in a particularly poor position: "You are therefore by your principles forced to deny the reality of sensible things, since you made it to consist in an absolute existence exterior to the mind. That is to say, you are a downright sceptic. So I have gained my point, which was to show your principles led to scepticism" (206–7). At this point Hylas is not sure what to believe. He asks Philonous for some time to consider what they have been discussing. They agree to meet the next day to continue their discussion.

NOTE

1 Berkeley makes this connection between impossibility and inconceivability in two ways. In the first draft Introduction to the *Principles* he states that if we hold that what is impossible can be conceived, this entails that we can conceive of things that God cannot create, which Berkeley takes to be an absurdity (*Works* 2:125). Another defence of this relation between impossibility and inconceivability is found in the first two editions (but not the final, third edition) of *Alciphron*

VII (*Works* 3:333–4) and in *A Defence of Free-Thinking in Mathematics* (§46). Here he connects impossibility and inconceivability with the idea of contradiction. The idea is that if something is impossible, then it involves a contradiction; and if something involves a contradiction, then it cannot be conceived. For Locke's endorsement of this view see *Essay* 3.10.33, 4.7.9 (which Berkeley cites in *New Theory* §125). Baxter (1997: 207–8n1) makes an interesting case for resisting this 'Berkeleyan' interpretation of these passages in Locke.

FURTHER READING

Locke's account of the primary/secondary quality distinction and its philosophical import has been widely discussed. An influential paper is Michael Jacovides (1999), "Locke's resemblance theses" *Philosophical Review*, 108 (4): 461–96. John Mackie, *Problems from Locke* (Clarendon Press 1976), chapter 2, argued that Berkeley misunderstood the distinction. Barry Stroud (1980), "Berkeley v. Locke on primary qualities" *Philosophy*, 55 (212): 149–66; Margaret Wilson, "Did Berkeley completely misunderstand the basis of the primary-secondary quality distinction in Locke?" in Colin M. Turbayne (ed.) *Berkeley: Critical and Interpretive Essays* (University of Minnesota Press 1982); and Lisa Downing "Sensible qualities and secondary qualities in the first dialogue" in Stefan Storrie (ed.), *Berkeley's Three Dialogues: New Essays* (Oxford University Press 2018), have come to Berkeley's defence.

For a defence of Locke's theory of abstraction against Berkeley's criticism see John Mackie (1976), chapter 4, and C. C. W. Taylor (1978), "Berkeley's theory of abstract ideas" *Philosophical Quarterly*, 28: 97–115. This has been challenged by John Roberts, *A Metaphysics for the Mob: The Philosophy of George Berkeley* (2007), chapter 2. Detailed interpretations of Berkeley's understanding of abstraction can be found in Julius Weinberg, *Abstraction, Relation, and Induction* (University of Wisconsin Press 1965), chapter 1; Kenneth Winkler, *Berkeley: An Interpretation* (Clarendon Press 1989), chapter 2; and Sam Rickless "The relation between anti-abstractionism and idealism in Berkeley's metaphysics" *British Journal for the History of Philosophy*, 20 (4): 723–40.

The classic account of Berkeley's master argument is Andre Gallois (1974), "Berkeley's master argument" *Philosophical Review*, 83 (1): 55–69. For a recent sophisticated discussion see Sam Rickless,

Berkeley's Argument for Idealism (Oxford University Press 2013), chapter 3.

The Arnauld–Malebranche controversy has been examined by Russell Wahl (1988), "The Arnauld–Malebranche controversy and Descartes' ideas" *The Monist*, 71 (4): 560–72; and Denis Moreau, "The Malebranche–Arnauld debate" in Steven M. Nadler (ed.), *The Cambridge Companion to Malebranche* (Cambridge University Press 2000), pp. 87–111.

Adverbial readings of Berkeley are found in George Pitcher (1969), "Minds and ideas in Berkeley" *American Philosophical Quarterly*, 6 (3): 198–207; Margaret Atherton (1983), "The coherence of Berkeley's theory of mind" *Philosophy and Phenomenological Research*, 43 (3): 389–99; and Melissa Frankel (2013), "Acts, ideas, and objects in Berkeley's metaphysics" *Canadian Journal of Philosophy*, 43 (4): 475–93. Criticisms of this view have been put forward by Kenneth Winkler, *Berkeley: An Interpretation* (Clarendon Press 1989), chapter 9, and Jennifer Smalligan Marušić, "Berkeley on the objects of perception" in Stefan Storrie (ed.), *Berkeley's Three Dialogues: New Essays* (Oxford University Press 2018), pp. 40–60. 'Object' theories, or perhaps better, 'anti-act' theories have been presented by Tom Stoneham, *Berkeley's World* (Oxford University Press 2002), chapter 3; Tom Stoneham, "Some issues in Berkeley's account of sense perception" in Stefan Storrie (ed.), *Berkeley's Three Dialogues: New Essays* (Oxford University Press 2018), pp. 24–39; and Marušić (2018).

5

THE EXISTENCE AND ACTIVITY OF GOD

Every sensation of mine which happens in Consequence of the general, known Laws of nature & is from without i.e. independent of my Will demonstrates the Being of a God. i.e. of an unextended incorporeal Spirit which is omniscient, omnipotent etc.

Notebooks §838

When our protagonists meet the next day at the opening of the second dialogue Hylas concedes that he is a sceptic with regard to sensible things. But he is not ready to concede defeat in his competition with Philonous. Instead he declares a draw. His only comfort, he states, is that Philonous is in an equally miserable position. Philonous denies being a sceptic with regard to sensible things. Hylas expresses surprise at this. How can one employ staples from the arguments of the sceptical canon and still deny such conclusions? Philonous explains that the sceptical conclusion is premised on the belief that the reality of sensible things consists in an absolute existence independently of being perceived. Since he is not burdened by this supposition, he does not need to draw the sceptical conclusion at this point. Instead,

Philonous is happy to accept that the reality of sensible things depends on their being perceived by a mind. This is his starting point for building up a new and positive account of the structure of reality. Instead of denying the reality of the sensible world because it depends on being perceived, he assumes that the sensible world is just as it appears and then considers what follows from that. The first consequence is that, since the world does not depend on my mind, or any other human mind, for its existence, it must depend on an infinite omnipresent mind that contains and supports the entire sensible world. In other words, Philonous maintains that the nature of the sensible discussed in the first dialogue is a premise for the conclusions, first, that God exists, and, second, that God is the reality that underpins the sensible world.

Hylas' immediate response to this claim sets the agenda for the second dialogue: "What! This is no more than I and all Christians hold; nay, and all others too who believe there is a God, and that he knows and comprehends all things" (213). Hylas is not merely a materialist, he also believes in a Christian God. Accordingly, the debate turns towards the relation between God and material substance. Specifically, the second dialogue has the following structure. First they debate Philonous' claim that his immaterialist position gives a sure proof of the existence of God. Then they consider the claim that immaterialism is a more rigorous and simple theory of the relation between God and the sensible world than any theory that includes material substance. Finally, they consider Philonous' claim that all conceivable theories of material substance are either false or incoherent. This chapter will consider the first claim, the second and third will be addressed in the next chapter.

A DIGRESSION

The second dialogue begins with a little episode that does not fit in with the broader narrative. The objection that Hylas puts forward here is, however, of considerable interest so we will consider it briefly before moving on to the main theme of the dialogue. Hylas suggests that modern science has the solution to his predicament. Its explanation for how we come to have ideas does not appeal to the mind but only to material things. So it is within the sphere of scientific theory that we find the proof for the existence of material substance. In short, the view is that we are affected by outer objects in the nerve endings of our sensory organs. These nerves send signals, 'vibratory motions', to the brain, which in turn, and wholly mechanically, cause sensations. At the time Berkeley wrote the *Three Dialogues*, our knowledge of the human nervous system and the brain was limited, and Hylas would, no doubt, come up with a more sophisticated or at least more detailed account today, but the basics would be pretty much the same.

Philonous' answer is that the brain is itself a sensible thing. It is a gray, gooey thing with a certain shape, weight, etc. It follows that the brain is an idea and exists only in the mind. Can an idea be the cause or occasion of another idea? If so, what is the nature and origin of this primary idea – the brain? On the model that Hylas has presented, the 'vibratory motions', which are themselves ideas, cause activity in the brain, which is another idea, and this in turn causes sensations, or so many other ideas. On this view, then, the cause of sensations is itself a sensation, which is not an explanation at all.

ON THE DOCTRINE OF SEEING ALL THINGS IN GOD

While Hylas does not presently believe in the reality of sensible things, he does believe in the existence of God and in material substance. Philonous believes in the reality of sensible things and in the existence of God, but not in material substance. Philonous states that these differences amount to quite heterogeneous ways of conceiving of God, while Hylas does not initially see the discrepancies. He asks: "But so long as we all believe the same thing, what matter is it how we come by that belief?" (212). The belief in question is that God perceives all things. However, Philonous immediately points out two differences in their views. The first point is the obvious metaphysical difference, namely that, according to the materialist position, material things subsist regardless of whether they are perceived or not. The second point is the epistemological point that the grounds for believing in the existence of God are different for the theological materialist than for the immaterialist. As Philonous characterizes the materialist position, it starts with positing God, and then concludes that he perceives all things. The immaterialist, on the other hand, begins by upholding that sensible things really exist, that is, that they are necessarily perceived, and then infer that there is an infinite mind that perceives the entire world. In this way, immaterialism contains within it a direct proof for the existence of God. According to Philonous, the standard argument for God's existence is the argument from design, which proves "from the beauty and usefulness of the several parts of the creation, that it was the workmanship of God" (212). While Philonous thinks this is a wonderful argument, it requires long digressions into astronomy and other sciences to convince the non-believer, and might therefore be less forceful than the direct argument afforded by immaterialism. Hylas is impressed by the epistemological advantage of immaterialism but seeks clarification on the metaphysical issue. In particular he wants to understand how Philonous' view of the relation between the world and God compares to the view put forward by Malebranche, that we 'see all things in God'. Philonous' reply, which was greatly extended in the 1734 edition of the work, is to say that on a very general level he agrees with the union with God that seems to be suggested by Malebranche's view, which Philonous characterizes by the saying of Paul in Acts 17:28 "that in God we live, and move, and have our being" (214). But there the similarities end, and, in fact, he takes his position to be diametrically opposed to Malebranche's on all relevant philosophical issues. Berkeley rarely explicitly engages with another philosopher at such length in his early writings, there are, however obvious reasons why he would do this with Malebranche in the *Three Dialogues*.

The association of Berkeley with Malebranche suggested itself to many readers of the *Principles* at the time. As we saw in Chapter 1, Percival reported that Clarke and Whiston "wished you had employed your thoughts less on metaphysics, ranking you with Father Malebranche, Norris and another whose name I have forgot".[1] Berkeley replied on 27 November that "I think the notions I embrace are not in the least coincident with, or agreeing with, theirs, but indeed plainly inconsistent with them in the main points, insomuch that I know few writers whom I take myself at bottom to differ more from than them" (McCracken & Tipton 2000: 164–5). This perception of Berkeley's immaterialism persisted throughout the 1700s despite Berkeley's efforts in the *Three Dialogues*. As Bracken (1959) McCracken and Tipton (2000), and Storrie (2013) have shown, this was in great part due to Father Tournemine and the other editors of the journal *Mémoires de Trévoux* who sought to implicate dubious views to Malebranche by associating him with a misrepresentation of Berkeley as a solipsist and moral egoist. Here is a passage from the 1713 review of the *Three Dialogues*, which gives a taste of the polemic:

> "Mr. Berkley [sic] continues to sustain obstinately that there are no bodies and that the material world is only an intelligible world; he crushes the new philosophers through their own principles. I. Extension, he says, has no more existence than the sensible qualities, it is only an idea in our spirit. II. One sees bodies only in God, it is therefore useless for them to exist outside of God"
>
> (Mémoires de Trévoux, December 1713: 2198–9).

These considerations weighed heavily on Berkeley's mind when he composed the second dialogue and Hylas challenges Philonous to distinguish his view from Malebranche in detail. Hylas summarizes the Malebranchian view that we see all things in God in the following way:

> *H:* They conceive that the soul, being immaterial, is incapable of being united with material things, so as to perceive them in themselves, but that she perceives them by her union with the substance of God, which being spiritual is therefore purely intelligible, or capable of being the immediate object of a spirit's thought. Besides, the divine essence contains in it perfections correspondent to each created being, and which are for that reason proper to exhibit or represent them to the mind. (214)

As Hylas characterizes Malebranche, he is a follower of Descartes who sees a radical distinction between mind and body as two distinct created substances. This metaphysical divide between mind and matter is also emphasized in Malebranche's epistemology. Because they differ in kind, the mind cannot be in direct contact with matter. The mind can only be in direct contact with something spiritual, not with material substance. Therefore, to have veridical knowledge of the material world Malebranche believes that perception is understood as a "union with the substance of God, which being spiritual is therefore purely intelligible, or capable of being the immediate object of a spirit's thought" (213).

Philonous begins his criticism of Malebranche by stating that in avoiding the difficulties posed by the interaction between mental substance and material substance, Malebranche runs into other difficulties. The ideas we have of physical objects are perfectly inert and consisting of parts and divisible into parts. But the substance that is God is the complete opposite. It is a "purely active being" that is "indivisible" (214). It therefore does not seem that our ideas can be about God at all, as our sensory ideas are not the right kind of thing to represent or in any way be in the likeness of God. In one sense Malebranche would disagree with this characterization of ideas. For, according to him, ideas are not properties of finite minds, or modes of finite minds. Instead, ideas, for him, are God's ideas, which are infinite, immutable archetypes of the created world. What our minds access when connected to God is then properly something that is compatible with God's nature.

In another sense, however, Malebranche could be pressed on the issue that Philonous raises. While Malebranche does submit to the enthusiasm of an almost mystical union with God characteristic of Platonism, he is, at the same time, deeply pessimistic about the capacities of the human mind, which is "not a light unto himself". He emphasizes instead its complete dependence on the "light of universal Reason", again associated with Neoplatonism and particularly with Malebranche's main point of reference besides Descartes, namely Augustine (Dialogue 3, OC 12:64; JS 32). As he expresses it at one point:

> You are then actually seeing the divine substance, for that alone is visible or capable of enlightening the mind. But you do not see it in itself or as it really is. You see it only in its relation to material creatures, only as it is participable by or representative of them. Consequently, it is not strictly speaking God whom you see, but only the matter he can produce.
>
> (Dialogue 2, OC 12:51; JS 21)

Accordingly, when we look at God, all we really see is matter. This raises a host of issues, related to Philonous' original concern. Matter is itself divisible, passive, and finite and, like Philonous' sensible ideas, bears no resemblance to God. It is therefore hard to make sense of the claim that we see all things in God when what we see is the complete opposite of God. Philonous also notes that Malebranche's position, being "liable to all the absurdities of the common hypothesis [of the existence of material substance]" is susceptible to the scepticism that Hylas at present subscribes to. In addition, because of Malebranche's insistence on the natural world's and the human mind's utter dependence on God, both causally and cognitively, "it makes the material world serve no purpose" (214).

PHILONOUS' PROOF OF GOD'S EXISTENCE

Instead of the 'seeing all things in God' doctrine, Philonous present a different account of the relation between God and the sensible world:

> *P:* Take here in brief my meaning. It is evident that the things I per-
> ceive are my own ideas, and that no idea can exist unless it be
> in a mind. Nor is it less plain that these ideas or things by me
> perceived, either themselves or their archetypes, exist indepen-
> dently of my mind, since I know myself not to be their author, it
> being out of my power to determine at pleasure what particular
> ideas I shall be affected with upon opening my eyes or ears.
> They must therefore exist in some other mind, whose will it
> is they should be exhibited to me. [. . .] And from the variety,
> order, and manner of these [sensible impressions] I conclude
> the Author of them to be wise, powerful, and good, beyond
> comprehension. (214–15)

Philonous' qualification that this is his argument "in brief" should be acknowledged here. There are a number of suppressed premises that that are only discussed later in the dialogues, as we shall see. On a general level the argument consists of three parts. The first part concerns the nature of the sensible things and specifically the claim that they are mind-dependent ideas. The second part specifies the right kind of perceiver required for ideas to exist, a mind different from my mind. The third part concerns the features of the mind identified in the second part and aims to show the perfection of that mind.

The claim in the first part is the conclusion of the lengthy investigation into the nature of the sensible in the first dialogue. The second and third parts are what will concern us here and we will begin with the second part. The first thing to note is that it is a sharp turn away from the strict first-person perspective that Philonous fastened on in the first dialogue. There he argued that the existence of sensible qualities amounts to being perceived by *his* or another particular person's mind, identifying these qualities with *his* perceived pain and pleasure and noting the ever changing perceptions in *his* mind. These arguments suggest that sensible qualities depend for their existence on being perceived by me or some other finite perceiver.

But now he points to a completely different aspect of experience: "Nor is it less plain that these ideas or things by me perceived, either themselves or their archetypes, exist independently of my mind, since I know myself not to be their author" (214). Philonous is now stating that the sensible things that I perceive, while they do exist in my mind, do not really depend on me for their existence. This is "plain" because of the limitations of his will with regard to events in the universe. For since all sensible things are ideas, but I am not able to control and determine what sensible things will appear or in what order they will appear, they are not dependent on me. For example, when I open my eyes I do not choose what I will see, and, regardless of how much I focus my will, this table in front of me will not start levitating. This impotency of the human mind is codified into our understanding of the difference between imagination and sensation. Through our imagination we are able to conjure up, more or less, whatever ideas we want. But these ideas are only in *our* minds and do not interact with sensible things.

If we accept that sensible things must be perceived to exist and that they do not depend on my mind for their existence, the next issue is what it means for a mind or spirit to perceive a sensible thing such that it exists. Specifically, if there is a mind that perceives all sensible things, is it active or passive in perceiving? Does it merely maintain sensible things in existence by passively perceiving them, or does it create the things it perceives? As Philonous indicates in the passage quoted above, he understands God to be the "author" of our ideas and therefore his must be the latter position. However, it is a central feature of the theory of sense perception that Philonous has defended at length in the end of the first dialogue, that the mind is entirely passive when it perceives. How can Philonous show that the infinite mind that encompasses the entire universe is one that actively creates rather than one that merely passively perceives all things? As Rickless (2018) has shown, we find the answer in the third dialogue. There Hylas presses Philonous on his conception of God and asks what right he has to claim that what he calls God is properly speaking a mind, capable of both willing and understanding:

> *P:* I assert as well as you that since we are affected from without, we must allow powers to be without in a being distinct from ourselves. So far we are agreed. But then we differ as to the kind of this powerful being. [. . .] Thus I prove it to be spirit. From the effects I see produced, I conclude there are actions; and because actions, volitions; and because there are volitions, there must be a will. (240)

In this passage Philonous begins by stating that he and Hylas agree that the sensations that affect us have a distinct cause, but that they disagree about whether this external thing is matter or mind. The options they choose as possible candidates show a further agreement. Neither of them argue that sensible things can themselves be the causes of our sensations. As we saw in the first dialogue, Hylas aimed to locate the power of objects in insensible primary qualities. Philonous' reasons for maintaining that sensible things are inert is that sensible things are nothing but ideas and ideas are "passive and inert" (213). In the *Three Dialogues* Philonous merely assumes this, presumably because it is accepted by his philosophical opponent, but in *Principles* 25 he presents the following argument. Ideas exist only in the mind, therefore there is nothing to an idea beside that of which we can be aware. When we examine our ideas we find that ideas cannot by themselves do or produce anything, therefore there is truly no power or activity in them. Ideas, being inactive, cannot be the causes of our affections. Therefore, the cause must be something active.

The next step in the argument is the claim that action entails volition. As Philonous states a few lines up from the above quote, "I have no notion of any action distinct from volition" (239). The idea is that the only model of causal activity available to us is one according to which ideas in our minds are produced through imagination, and, because "I have a mind to have some notion or meaning in what I say" (239) the causal activity of creating sensible ideas can only be modelled on the notion of an act of will.

Berkeley, then, provides two separate arguments. One argument, which occurs at 214–15 and elsewhere, defends the existence of an understanding that perceives all sensible things, and another argument at 239–40 defends the existence of a will, which accounts for the changing sensible things that affect me. After presenting the will argument, Philonous triumphantly declares:

P: Again, the things I perceive must have an existence, they or
their archetypes, out of my mind; but being ideas, neither they
nor their archetypes can exist otherwise than in an understanding. There is therefore an understanding. But will and
understanding constitute in the strictest sense a mind or spirit.
The powerful cause, therefore, of my ideas is in strict propriety
of speech a spirit. (240)

Now, however, we could present a challenge to Philonous. Despite
his two arguments showing that (1) an understanding perceives all
sensible things and (2) all sensible things are caused by a will, he
has not shown that the understanding and the will belong to the same
entity. He has not argued, but merely asserted, that a spirit, meaning a
unified being with both understanding and will, is responsible for the
creation and perception of the sensible universe.

As Winkler (1985, 1989) and Rickless (2018) have shown, in order to
conclude that the willing and the perceiving entity are the same unified
spirit Philonous is most likely relying on another assumption, which was
common though by no means ubiquitous at the time. This is the rejection
of 'blind agency', that there can be no volition without perception. For
example, Descartes, in a letter to Regius, stated about human beings that
"we cannot will anything without understanding what we will" (CSMK
III 182; AT III 372). Likewise, Malebranche, taking on the divine perspective, held that "God must have within Himself the ideas of all the
beings He has created (since otherwise He could not have created them)"
(*Search* 3.2.6, 230). Locke, in his correspondence with Limborch, which
Berkeley studied intently and commented on in his *Notebooks*, wrote:

If you say that the judgement of the understanding, or cogitation, is
not one of the 'requisites for acting'. Please consider whether, while
you want in this way to make a man free, you are not simply making
him a blind agent; and whether, in order to make him free, you are
not taking away from him understanding, without which any sort of
Liberty cannot exist or be supposed to exist.

(Correspondence 7.407)

Locke is here interested in showing that free will requires an understanding of what one wills, or else one is acting 'blindly'. At a very

general level though, what all three of the above quoted authors are stating is that volition must have some content, there must be some conception of what is sought when one wills.

In his *Notebooks* Berkeley affirmed this principle repeatedly. At entry 545, for example, where he writes "Distinct from or without perception there is no volition". In the *Three Dialogues* Philonous gets closest to endorsing this when he says that "a thing which hath no ideas in itself, cannot impart them to me" (239). For this to not be met by the obvious rejoinder that a stone by landing on my foot can impart the idea of pain without having the idea of pain or any other ideas, it seems plausible that Philonous is assuming that by "imparting" an idea to me should be understood as willing that the idea is had by me. In that case Philonous' point is that willing has content in terms of ideas. Philonous' argument for a will that causes sensible ideas and his denial of blind agency then leads to the conclusion that this will must also perceive what is being willed. Therefore, the will that causes sensible ideas in me and the understanding that perceives all things in the sensible universe belong to the same entity, and an entity that is both will and understanding is by definition a mind or spirit.

This is, in broad outline, how Philonous establishes the second part of the argument, that all sensible things that I perceive are brought about by a mind. The next step is to use this conclusion as a premise for an argument that the mind that causes these ideas is God. Rickless (2013, 2018) has examined this move in great detail and the following exposition is largely based on his approach.

Philonous' central argument for the conclusion that the mind that is responsible for the existence of sensible ideas is all-powerful, all-knowing and completely good is found in the beginning of the third dialogue, where he states:

> P: When I deny sensible things an existence out of the mind, I do not mean my mind in particular, but all minds. Now it is plain they have an existence exterior to my mind, since I find them by experience to be independent of it. There is therefore some other mind wherein they exist, during the intervals between the times of my perceiving them, as likewise they did before my birth and would do after my supposed annihilation. And as the same is

true with regard to all other finite created spirits, it necessarily
follows, there is an omnipresent eternal Mind, which knows and
comprehends all things and exhibits them to our view in such a
manner, and according to such rules as he himself has ordained,
and are by us termed the 'laws of nature'. (230–1)

Philonous' reasoning for his conclusion is based on three claims. The
first point Philonous makes is that because sensible things are independent of finite minds perceiving them, sensible things must exist
continuously "in the intervals between the times of my perceiving
them, as likewise they did before my birth and would do after my
supposed annihilation". Why should we think that sensible things
exist when we are not perceiving them? One possibility could be that
Philonous thinks that this is a reasonable inference from best explanation based on the following considerations. The world we experience
is stable and coherent. If I see something, then close my eyes momen-
tarily and then look again, things will typically look the way they did
before. The view that sensible things continue to exist when I do not
perceive them is a better explanation of the stability and coherence
of the world than the view that sensible things go in and out of existence intermittently. Archaeological artefacts and geological research
also strongly suggests that sensible things have been in existence long
before my birth and presumably will continue to exist long after my
death. This claim will be examined in more detail in Chapter 7 when
we consider Philonous' discussion of the 'continuity' of the sensible
world in the third dialogue.

The second point introduces a new element into the argument.
In the second dialogue, Philonous was content to draw conclusions
about a mind perceiving the sensible ideas that *he* perceived. Now he
wants to extend his reasoning to take into consideration the situation
of "all other finite created spirits". One thing that is true of all such
beings, regardless of whether they are mites or dogs or aliens of various kinds, is that they perceive ideas of which they are not causally
responsible, they perceive a limited number of such ideas, and they
experience the ideas as being in a certain order that is to some extent
predictable and lawful. The mind that is responsible for the existence
of sensible things must, therefore, be a mind that perceives all the
things that all finite minds perceive and, because sensible things exist

continuously, the infinite mind must also perceive all the sensible things that no finite mind perceives. This latter category of sensible things is itself infinite because the universe is (at least potentially) infinite, as Philonous explains: "But neither sense nor imagination are big enough to comprehend the boundless extent with all its glittering furniture. Though the labouring mind exert and strain each power to its utmost reach, there still stands out ungrasped a surplusage immeasurable" (211).

The third point is that the sensible ideas comprehended by the infinite mind are not only infinite in number but are ordered and display themselves with perfect lawfulness, harmony and beauty. While the first two points establish that the mind responsible for the existence of sensible things is infinitely powerful, the sheer number of sensible things does not, by itself, establish that the mind is infinitely wise and good. To establish this, Philonous can again be seen as proceeding by an inference from the best explanation. Only an infinite being with limitless power, foresight, and goodness could create such a world.

Philonous presents an argument for the existence of God that depends in part on the immaterialist conception of sensible things that he presented in the first dialogue, and on a number of observations about the degree of control that finite beings have over their sense perceptions, the structure of volition, and several inferences from observations about the extent and structure of the universe. One interesting feature of this argument in the context of the dialogues is that here Philonous and Hylas are broadly and without much controversy in agreement. Hylas also believes in the existence of God and is impressed by the way Philonous proceeds to argue for that thesis on the basis of his immaterialist philosophy.

NOTE

1   John Norris (1657–1711), an English follower of Malebranche.

FURTHER READING

The attempts to align Berkeley's immaterialism with Malebranche's philosophy have been documented by Harry Bracken, *The Early*

Reception of Berkeley's Immaterialism, 1710–1733 (Martinus Nijhoff 1959). On a more general level, Charles McCracken and Ian Tipton (eds), *Berkeley's Principles and Dialogues: Background Source Materials* (Cambridge University Press 2000) provides a helpful compendium of background sources and early reactions to Berkeley's thought.

Jonathan Bennett (1965), "Berkeley and God" *Philosophy*, 15: 207–21, and *Locke, Berkeley, Hume: Central Themes* (Clarendon Press 1971) is responsible for establishing the framework for most subsequent discussion about Berkeley's various proofs for the existence of God. Sam Rickless, "Berkeley's argument for the existence of God in the *Three Dialogues*" in Stefan Storrie (ed.), *Berkeley's Three Dialogues: New Essays* (Oxford University Press 2018) offers a detailed analysis of Berkeley's approach to the issue in the *Three Dialogues*. An in-depth account of the issues around 'blind agency' is given in Kenneth Winkler, *Berkeley: An Interpretation* (Clarendon Press 1989), chapter 7.

6

THE REJECTION OF THEISTIC MATERIALISM

The philosophers lose their Matter. The Mathematicians lose their insensible sensations, the profane their extended Deity. Pray what do the rest of Mankind lose, as for bodies &c we have them still.

Notebooks §391

Upon hearing Philonous' argument for the existence of God Hylas exclaims:

H: I think I understand you very clearly; and own the proof you give of a Deity seems no less evident than it is surprising. But allowing that God is the supreme and universal cause of all things, yet may not there be still a third nature besides spirits and ideas? May we not admit a subordinate and limited cause of our ideas? In a word, may there not for all that be matter?

P: How often must I inculcate the same thing? You allow the things immediately perceived by sense to exist nowhere without the mind; but there is nothing perceived by sense, which is not perceived immediately. Therefore there is nothing sensible that exists without the mind. The matter, therefore, which you still insist on is something intelligible, I suppose, something that may be discovered by reason and not by sense. (215)

Hylas first congratulates Philonous on his argument for the existence of God, and in particular for the conception of God as the "supreme and universal cause of all things" but still wants to consider if there is conceptual room for material substance as a "subordinate and limited cause of our ideas". In this way, Hylas wants to consider whether some form of theistic materialism, which maintains that God is the basis for the existence of all things, but which also leaves room for material substance to do some explanatory work in a complete account of the sensible world, is possible. Philonous' immediate response is to specify the conceptual space that this discussion will inhabit. As they have already agreed that all sensible things are mind-dependent, material substance will not be inferred from sensible things, but discovered by reason.

HYLAS' FOUR ACCOUNTS OF MATTER

Hylas' guiding thought in this part of the dialogue is that matter functions as an intermediate "third nature" between God and ideas. In this way he aims to carve out some conceptual space for matter to challenge Philonous' theistic immaterialism, which does not allow for any entity between mind(s) and ideas. This approach has a very long history, possibly first explicitly discussed by Plato in his dialogue *Timaeus*. In his account of the fundamental structure of the cosmos at least two categories of things are included. Stable intelligible natures that possess being, and changing sensible things that are in a state of perpetual becoming. After establishing this, Plato introduces a "third kind" (Plato *Timaeus* 49a), which is called the 'receptacle'. The receptacle is introduced as a substrate of sensible things, so they can be designated as something while in a state of becoming. "Its nature is to be available for anything to make its impression upon, and it is modified, shaped, and reshaped by the things that enter it. These are the things that make it appear different at different times" (50c). What Plato is describing here has been variously understood as 'matter' or as 'space', or as both, and has served as a starting point for the discussion of matter that developed through Aristotle, the Neoplatonists, scholastic philosophy and up to the early modern period. It is my contention that Berkeley is looking at this broad tradition when he has Hylas and Philonous discuss theological materialism.

Hylas' idea is that matter functions in a way that is modelled on the idea of a cause of ideas. Indeed, his first suggestion is that matter is a 'secondary cause' of ideas. However, as his position is presented with what seem to be insurmountable difficulties, Hylas gradually weakens his conception of the role of matter, from 'cause' to 'instrument', from 'instrument' to 'occasion', and finally from 'occasion' to 'something in general'.

Hylas' gives the following rationale for positing matter as a causal intermediary between God and ideas:

> H: I find myself affected with various ideas, whereof I know I am
>   not the cause; neither are they the cause of themselves, or of
>   one another, or capable of subsisting by themselves, as being
>   altogether inactive, fleeting, dependent beings. They have
>   therefore some cause distinct from me and them, of which I
>   pretend to know no more than that it is 'the cause of my ideas'.
>   And this thing, whatever it be, I call matter. (216)

The argument starts by noting that we are affected by various ideas. As Philonous explained in his argument for the existence of God, the cause of these ideas can lie neither with himself (because they are independent of him) nor with other ideas (since ideas are known to be inert from observation). Hylas' next step is designed to avoid the problems that arise from linking matter with sensible things, which he encountered when trying to formulate a conception of material substance in the first dialogue. He now says that he does not "pretend to know" what this cause is, most notably, he refuses to assign any sensible qualities to the cause. Instead, he holds that the cause, whatever its characteristics or properties might be, is what he calls 'matter'.

This argument uses the same premises that Philonous used to argue for the existence of a mind distinct from himself, which is responsible for the existence of his ideas. What is it about Hylas' notion of 'matter' that makes it different from a mind? Philonous presses Hylas on his issues when he says: "I do by no means find fault with your reasoning, in that you collect a cause from the phenomena; but I deny that the cause deducible by reason can properly be termed 'matter'" (216). Philonous challenges Hylas to say something more about matter than his guarded minimal account provides, which will allow him to distinguish matter from mind. Hylas response is to first accept that, of course, God is an infinite spirit and supreme cause of all things, but that matter, as an intermediary between God and ideas, plays a role as limited cause. Matter is capable of acting in this way because, though it has nothing in it of a spiritual nature, such as will and understanding, it is able to act by means of motion. Philonous' response to this is to state that motion is a sensible quality and that it is therefore entirely passive and can play no role as a cause for anything in nature. Hylas concedes that this is the case, stating: "when I stir my finger, it remains passive; but my will which produced the motion, is active" (217). The only kind of action we can conceive of, Philonous continues, is volition. Therefore, the only kind of cause that we can conceive of is mind or spirit.

Not deterred by this setback, Hylas launches into his second, slightly weaker, conception of material substance as an instrument: "But though matter may not be a cause, yet what hinders its being an instrument subservient to the supreme agent in the production of our ideas?" (217). The idea of an instrumental intermediary between God and natural events has a long and interesting history. It is found in the early (800 CE) Arabic Neoplatonist philosopher Al-Kindī's distinction between 'proximate' and 'remote' efficient causes.

> The one who shoots the arrow is the remote cause of killing the animal, whereas the arrow is the proximate cause of its being killed; for the one who shoots with the intention of killing the animal produces the piercing action of the arrow, but the arrow produces the killing of the living thing by wounding it and by [causing] the living thing to receive an effect from the arrow when it strikes.
>
> *(The Explanation of the Proximate Efficient Cause for Generation and Corruption,* § 11)

Later, as scholastic philosophers sought to reconcile the Aristotelian view that natural events derive from accidental and substantial forms with the view that God is causally efficacious with regard to these events, the idea of an instrument of God was explored. The typical example was a person using a pen to write. The pen is the cause of the writing on the paper, but the pen can only be efficacious in this way because the agent uses it to produce that effect. The pen is only an intermediate and instrumental cause of the writing. Aquinas held that secondary causes could produce effects, though they could not do so merely by virtue of their own power, but required participation with the primary cause – God (QPG III.7, TA, 13:60). This view was vigorously challenged by, among others, Duns Scotus, William of Ockham, Francisco Suárez and Durandus. Durandus took a view closer to Hylas' 'causation' approach. Berkeley discussed his view in a letter to Johnson, in which he is characterized as holding that "the world [is] a machine like a clock, made and put in motion by God, but afterwards continuing to go of itself" (LJ 281).

In the early modern period the central mechanistic metaphor of the world as a machine (typically a very complex clock) made by God the watchmaker has more than a hint of the idea of the material world as an instrument of God. Another discussion that centred on the idea of an instrument of God in the natural world occurred in the Leibniz–Clarke correspondence (1715–16). Newton, in Query 28 of his *Optics* suggested that space itself was an instrument, in the sense that it was the sensory of God whereby he "sees the things themselves intimately, and thoroughly perceives them, and comprehends them wholly by their immediate presence to himself". Leibniz's first letter objected to this claim because it meant that God needs an instrument, a sense organ, to perceive things. This, he argued, is contrary to God's omnipotence. In their first three letters Clarke and Leibniz rather amusingly go back and forth on this issue, with Clarke trying to diffuse the implications by stating that sensory does not mean sense organ and Leibniz replying by quoting a dictionary stating the contrary.

In response to Hylas' claim that matter is God's instrument Philonous tries to set a now familiar trap: "An instrument, say you; pray what may be the figure, springs, wheels, and motions of that instrument?" (217). He challenges Hylas to characterize matter as an instrument on the model of a sensible thing like a watch, or other machine or tool. If Hylas takes the bait, then Philonous will be able to point out that characterized in this way matter is, in fact, sensible and therefore nothing but idea. Hylas is wary of this move, stating that he is not concerned with determining the substance or qualities of this instrument. Philonous tries the same trick in a slightly subtler way, claiming: "You are then of opinion, it is made up of unknown parts, that it has unknown motions, and an unknown shape" (218). But Hylas refuses to be drawn in. He simply denies that matter, as instrument, has any motion or figure at all, since as all these characteristics are sensible qualities.

Philonous' old tricks are not working and, therefore, he must try another approach. This is to consider the concept of an instrument in the most general sense (ignoring any sensible particulars) and argue that matter, understood as an instrument, is incompatible with the divine attributes, and therefore it is impossible that God has created material substance as an instrument for creating sensible things. Philonous argues that an essential characteristic for instruments is that they are employed in actions only when an act of will is not sufficient:

> P: Is it not common to all instruments that they are applied to the doing those things only, which cannot be performed by the mere act of our wills? Thus, for instance, I never use an instrument to move my finger because it is done by a volition. But I should use one, if I were to remove part of a rock or tear up a tree by the roots. Are you of the same mind? Or can you show any example where an instrument is made use of in producing an effect immediately depending on the will of the agent? (218–19)

I do not use an instrument to move my finger, since I can typically do this simply through an act of will. To remove a tree stump from my lawn, however, my act of willing that the roots be pulled out is, sadly, not enough, and I need a shovel, an axe and a saw and some hard work (where my will is very much employed). Philonous next states that since God is an all-perfect spirit, and the existence of all things depend directly on his will, he does not need any instrument. And if he does not need it, would he make use of it? As God is all-powerful he does not need matter as instrument to create anything, and since he is all wise he would not make something that he had no need of. It is true that at some points in his writings, in his later work *Siris* in particular, Berkeley does speak of God's instruments, but in those cases he means that God creates things for his creatures to use as instruments, not that God himself makes use of them.

Hylas is not prepared to give up yet. His third conception of material substance is 'occasion'. This is a view associated with Malebranche. Malebranche held that God is the only efficient cause for all events in the universe. This means that Malebranche agrees with Philonous that material substance cannot be a cause or an instrument, but they disagree on two further points. First, Malebranche took material substance to exist and to play a non-causal role in the unfolding of natural events. Second, whereas Malebranche took God to have a monopoly on causation, this is not the case for Philonous. According to Philonous, finite spirits are causally active through their will. This is the case both for the act of creating ideas through imagination and the act of volition that results in bodily motion. In contrast, on Malebranche's view, our volition to move our arm is not itself causally efficacious, but a mere occasion for God to move our arm. The difference in analysing human volition has important consequences for understanding moral responsibility, both with regard to God in respect of the so-called 'problem of evil' and also with regard to human moral obligation. Berkeley's moral philosophy will be considered in Chapter 8, here we will briefly look at Hylas and Philonous' discussion of the problem of evil before moving on to consider Hylas' attempt to characterize material substance as occasion.

In the third dialogue Hylas suggests that Philonous' account of God has made him, in a sense, too powerful, such that the evil in the world should be attributed to God's will: "in making God the immediate author of all the motions in nature, you make him the author of murder, sacrilege, adultery, and the like heinous sins" (236). Philonous replies that Hylas has misunderstood his account of God's power in two different ways. First, by making God the direct cause of sensible things, without intermediaries such as instruments and occasions, God is not more or less responsible for evil. If someone commits murder with her bare hands or with a gun does not change the moral classification of the act. Therefore, the problem Hylas presents is no more a problem for him than it is for Hylas. But is it a problem? Philonous does not think that it is because he does not afford God as much power and activity as Malebranche does but allows for a rich sense of human action, so all the morally evil actions human beings commit are properly their responsibility:

P: I have denied there are any other agents beside spirits; but this
     is very consistent with allowing to thinking rational beings,
     in the production of motions, the use of limited powers, ulti-
     mately indeed derived from God, but immediately under the
     direction of their own wills, which is sufficient to entitle them to
     all the guilt of their actions. (237)

Finally, Philonous explains that at any rate he does not take outward
actions themselves to be good or evil. This is suggested by the fact
that the same act, say of killing another human being, is sometimes
deemed morally permissible (in war, in some cases of self-defence)
and other times not. Therefore, and here Philonous is lending a helping
hand to strong views of God's power such as Malebranche's, even if
God is the immediate cause of all physical actions, this does not make
him the "author of sin" (237).

Returning to the second dialogue, Hylas defines 'occasion' as "an
inactive unthinking being, at the presence whereof God excites ideas in
our minds" (220). He motivates his belief in the existence of such 'occasions' by stating: "When we see ideas produced in our minds after an
orderly and constant manner, it is natural to think they have some fixed
and regular occasions, at the presence of which they are excited" (220).
Hylas' view is characterized in terms of occasions being present to God
and God causing events at the presence of those occasions. To put it
crudely, occasions are like post-it notes we might have on our fridge
reminding us to, say, buy more milk. The post-it was written by me at a
different point in time and the note is not the cause of new milk appearing in the fridge, I caused that by going to the shop and so on. But the
post-it note being present to me in the morning is part of the story of why
I went to get the milk. Philonous first asks whether God perceives the
occasions and Hylas answers that he does, "otherwise they could not be
to him an occasion of acting" (220). God is, then, in some sense acting
on these perceptions, similarly to my acting on the reminder I left myself
to buy more milk. God is, therefore, influenced by this external object.
But, as Philonous points out, if God is all-powerful and all-knowing,
he should not need any kind of 'reminder' to act.

We might want to understand occasions in a weaker sense, as
merely assuming that there is something in respect to which God
deliberates when acting. After all, as we saw in Chapter 5 it is crucial

to Philonous' account of God that he is not a 'blind agent'. Indeed, Philonous presumably refers to that earlier discussion when he speaks of "my allowing that there are certain things perceived by the mind of God, which are to Him the occasion of producing ideas in us" (220). These ideas in God's mind are what he calls 'archetypes'. On this view Hylas' mistake is just that he inferred from this that the things perceived by God are material substances. On Philonous' view these occasions should be understood to be ideas in God's mind, thus avoiding introducing a problematic intermediate 'third nature' between mind and idea.

ON THE LIMITS OF THOUGHT AND MEANING

Hylas is once again at sea. He is not prepared to give up his belief in material substance, but, at the same time, he takes all possible grounds for such a belief to have been removed. Hylas' way of thinking about the issue now leads the discussion into a new phase, but one that Philonous has been building up to for some time. When Hylas moves from his account of matter as 'cause' to matter as 'instrument', he moves from giving sensible attributes (in the case of 'cause' it was 'motion') to giving a partial definition or what we might call a conceptual attribute (in the case of instrument 'instrument in general', which turned out to include 'being applied when an act of will is insufficient'). In this transition from sensible to conceptual features, there is an interlude in which Hylas tries to maintain a purely negative conception of matter, as he says: "I do not pretend to have any notion of it" (218). In response to this, Philonous asks what reason Hylas has to believe that this unknown thing exists. Hylas wants to know why it is he who must adduce a reason to believe it exists and not Philonous' burden to show that he has some reason to believe that it doesn't exist. In reply to Hylas turning the tables Philonous states that in order not to believe in the existence of a thing, it is sufficient not to have any reason to believe in it. What this means is that in order to have warrant to believe in the existence of something, one must be able to produce some reason for why it exists. Philonous and Hylas are here talking about the limits of intelligibility. Specifically, they are considering what the minimum requirement is for asserting, with some form of content, that something exists. I have considered this move in some detail in Storrie (2018).

After giving up on matter as 'occasion' Hylas again pushes at the limits of intelligibility. Hylas explains that he is now in the following position:

> H: I acknowledge it is possible we might perceive all things just as we do now, though there was no matter in the world; neither can I conceive, if there be matter, how it should produce any idea in our minds. And I do farther grant, you have entirely satisfied me, that it is impossible there should be such a thing as matter in any of the foregoing acceptations. But still I cannot help supposing that there is matter in some sense or other. What that is I do not indeed pretend to determine. (221)

Hylas now accepts that material substance is not required for explaining our perception of the world, and that it cannot in fact account for our perceptions. These were his main reasons for belief in matter in the first dialogue. Further, he accepts that any content he has tried to give to the notion of material substance: 'cause', 'instrument' and 'occasion' are impossible because they contradict the divine attributes that are integral for his theological materialism.

He now decides that he understands by material substance nothing but an 'entity in general' which he characterizes as having no positive attribute or meaning attached to it at all:

> P: It seems then you include, in your present notion of matter, nothing but the general abstract idea of 'entity'.
> H: Nothing else, save only that I superadd to this general idea the negation of all those particular things, qualities, or ideas that I perceive, imagine, or in any wise apprehend. (222)

After being vigorously pressed to give a reason to believe in the existence of matter thus (un)conceived, we get the following exchange:

> P: I challenge you to show me that thing in nature which needs matter to explain or account for it.
> H: The reality of things cannot be maintained without supposing the existence of matter. And is not this, think you, a good reason why I should be earnest in its defence? (224)

Hylas' view is, then, that matter is something quality-less and unintelligible, and yet at the same time something that is necessary for the reality of sensible things. It is an indistinct intermediary between the steadfast intelligible and causal principle of the universe (God, according to his theological materialism) and the changeable sensible things; it is required to ground sensible things so that they don't simply float around in 'thin air', but rather so that they are the sensations *of* something. This dual aspect, its unknowability on the one hand and the confidence in its crucial function on the other hand, might strike some readers as paradoxical. It might further seem that Hylas is speaking out of desperation in that he has seen his more content-ful accounts defeated and is now retreating to a vague defensive stance. While it seems that Berkeley wants to portray the situation in that way, it also seems that this notion of material substance is of central importance because it is approximating the leading intuition of the conception of material substance that is at the heart of the classical presentation of the ontology of matter, namely Plato's 'receptacle' in the *Timaeus*, and also the notion of material substance in Descartes and Locke.

In the *Timaeus*, the receptacle is presented as a third kind of thing beside intelligible forms and sensible things, as the place and/or stuff in which sensible things undergo change. It is characterized as something that, because it takes on all forms of sensible existence, is itself "totally devoid of any characteristics" (50e) and can be likened to something that is indefinitely malleable such that any sensible impression can be moulded upon it, like wax (50e–51a). Because of this lack of fixed qualities it is "difficult and vague" (49a). Yet, as Hylas just stated, it is required to maintain the reality of sensible things. As Plato rather colourfully puts it:

> It [the "third kind"] is itself apprehended by a kind of bastard reasoning that does not involve sense perception, and it is hardly even an object of conviction. We look at it as in a dream when we say that everything that exists must of necessity be somewhere, in some place and occupying some space, and that which doesn't exist somewhere, whether on earth or in heaven, doesn't exist at all.
>
> (52b)

In *Meditations*, 2 (AT VII, 30–4, CMS 20–3) Descartes famously illustrates our epistemological situation with regard to matter with a piece of wax, which he generalizes to all physical objects. One of his points is that physical objects do not have fixed sensible properties that belong to them. A piece of wax that has just been taken from a honeycomb has a faint taste and smell of honey, a golden colour, a certain degree of solidity, shape and size. However, when Descartes puts the piece of wax by the fire, all its properties change and it becomes an odourless and tasteless liquid. What remains throughout this transformation is, Descartes believes, the capacity to have a size and shape, which he refers to as its 'extension'. This general ability to undergo countless changes in shape and size is a feature of the wax, or any physical object, that cannot be known by the senses because the senses only gives us the particular spatial determinations we perceive. It is also not known by the imagination for the similar reason that we can only imagine a finite number of shapes. The obscurity and difficulty in grasping the underlying material nature of things is felt by Descartes, as it was by Plato. But ultimately Descartes believes that extension is knowable through the intellect, though it is less distinctly known than the mind.

Locke rejected the notion of the intellect as the source of knowledge of the substrate of sensible qualities. As a consequence, he gave a more sceptical account of the nature of both material and mental substance than did Descartes:

> we have as clear a notion of the substance of spirit as we have of body: the one being supposed to be (without knowing what it is) the *substratum* to those simple ideas we have from without; and the other supposed (with a like ignorance of what it is) to be the *substratum* to those operations which we experiment in ourselves within. 'Tis plain then, that the idea of corporeal *substance* in matter, is as remote from our conceptions, and apprehensions, as that of spiritual *substance*, or *spirit*.
>
> (*Essay* 2.23.5)

Philonous does not think that we have the same clarity about the substance of body and spirit. As we will see in Chapter 8 when we turn to Philonous' account of the mind in the third dialogue, he thinks spirit can be known with all requisite clarity. While Locke does not offer much in the way of content to his physical and spiritual substratum, he offers more than Hylas' conception of a mere 'thing in general':

> The idea then we have, to which we give the general name substance, being nothing, but the supposed, but unknown support of those qualities, we find existing, which we imagine cannot subsist, *sine re substante*, without something to support them, we call that support *substantia*, which, according to the true import of the word, is in plain English, *standing under* or *upholding*.
>
> (*Essay* 2.23.2)

This is a 'thin' conception of material substance as an unknown something that 'supports' physical objects, but it is more than Hylas contends in his fourth account of matter as an unknown intermediary. Hylas does not avail himself of this notion of material substance here because it was in fact discussed and rejected in a passage in the first dialogue which we passed over in Chapter 4 but which is worth considering now. This passage begins with Hylas stating that he finds it necessary to suppose a material substratum because without it sensible things cannot be conceived to exist (197). Philonous' line of questioning proceeds like Descartes' musings about the piece of wax. First he asks Hylas whether he has a 'positive' notion of matter through the senses. Since Hylas denies that he has any such notion, Philonous next asks whether he has a 'positive' notion of it through reflection and reason. This is the avenue Descartes would have pursued, but Hylas also denies that he possesses this.

In the *Three Dialogues* it is not explained why this avenue would not be open to Hylas. In *Principles* 18 Berkeley explains that knowing material substance by reason is not possible because that would require a necessary connection between externally existing material objects and our perception of objects. For since the "patrons of matter" (it seems he has Descartes and Malebranche in mind here) hold that we could have the same experience we do now even if material substance did not exist, we cannot proceed logically from the concept of an object of experience to a mind-independent object.

Instead Hylas says that he has no positive idea of matter at all but only has a relative idea. This is the notion of matter as a 'support'. As we have seen, this is exactly the same as Locke's account of material (and spiritual) substratum as support. Furthermore, Locke explicitly holds that this is "[a]n obscure and *relative Idea* of Substance in general" (*Essay* 2.23.3 first emphasis mine). Locke explicitly understands his notion of substance to be merely relative, again Hylas agrees.

Philonous proceeds to attack this relative notion of 'substance' and 'substratum'. In order to have a relative notion of something, we must understand the relation (support) that that thing (material substance) has to something of which we have a positive notion (sensible thing). Philonous' point will be that we have no such understanding. The literal meaning of the Latin term 'substratum' is 'to spread or be strewn under'. Philonous then wonders if the substratum is extended. Hylas denies this because extension is a mode, that is to say, a defining property, of the substratum. Since the substratum 'supports' the properties that inhere in it, it cannot itself possess the properties it is supposed to support, for otherwise it just is the property, not the underlying basis for the property. But then Hylas' notion of substratum is a notion of an unextended 'spreading under', but this makes no literal sense, for it is impossible to conceive of a thing being spread without having extension. The relation of matter spreading under these sensible things is in no way clarified by referring to a nonliteral meaning of 'spread under'. At this point Hylas states that according to him 'substratum' does not signify its literal meaning, but that it is merely a synonym for 'substance'. Philonous then uses the same approach for this notion. The literal meaning of 'substance' in Latin is to 'stand under'. For something to stand under something else this something must be extended. But substance is the support for properties such as extension and therefore it cannot be extended. It is then not clear at all what this relation of 'standing under' could mean. Hylas again protests that the term should not be taken literally but has now run out of synonyms. The passage therefore ends with Hylas accepting that his relative conception of matter as support has no meaning:

> P: Pray let me know any sense, literal or not literal, that you understand it in. – How long must I wait for an answer, Hylas?
>
> H: I declare I know not what to say. I once thought I understood well enough what was meant by matter's supporting accidents. But now, the more I think on it the less can I comprehend it; in short, I find that I know nothing of it. (199)

Returning to the second dialogue, Hylas is now defending a notion of material substance that does not even include the Lockean relative notion of quasi-spatial 'support'. Instead Hylas' strategy is to not give any content whatsoever to the notion of material substance and in this way hold on to this belief because, being contentless, this 'notion' of material substance has no feature that can contradict any other belief or aspect of reality. In this way he hopes to avoid the problem that beset his first three accounts of material substance as intermediary. Philonous' response to this is to point out that Hylas is correct to hold that this account of material substance is not internally contradictory, and neither is it in conflict with any other aspect of Hylas' theological materialism. But ultimately this is not a victory for Hylas because if there is no positive or relative notion attached to the term at all, then the term has no meaning whatsoever, matter is just an empty word.

Philonous is now ready to present his response to the basic issue about what gives sensible things their reality, which led thinkers from Plato to Descartes to posit matter. As an example of a sensible thing he uses his glove:

P: But to fix on some particular thing; is it not a sufficient evidence to me of the existence of this glove, that I see it, and feel it, and wear it? Or if this will not do, how is it possible I should be assured of the reality of this thing, which I actually see in this place, by supposing that some unknown thing, which I never did or can see, exists after an unknown manner, in an unknown place, or in no place at all? How can the supposed reality of that which is intangible be a proof that anything tangible really exists? or of that which is invisible, that any visible thing, or in general of anything which is imperceptible, that a perceptible exists? Do but explain this, and I shall think nothing too hard for you. (224)

Philonous' point is that what makes sensible things real is internal to the sensible. We deem a sensible thing like a glove real because we can see and feel it and wear it. It does not stand in need of a non-sensible, imperceptible and passive thing to support it and uphold its reality. While this is a simple and straightforward answer, it is not clear that Hylas should be immediately persuaded by this account. Philonous' answer raises many further questions that matter has traditionally been posited to solve. The most pressing of these are the following. If the reality of sensible things just is to be perceived, then, as you and I perceive things differently, do we really perceive the same thing? What happens to things when no one perceives them? How do we distinguish what is real in experience from mere appearance? Having methodically attacked the notion of matter, Philonous must now start building up his own theory, and in doing so he must answer these and many other questions. Berkeley clearly saw the need for this and he has Hylas and Philonous explore these and many further issues in the third dialogue.

FURTHER READING

Sarah Broadie, *Nature and Divinity in Plato's Timaeus* (Cambridge University Press 2012), chapter 6, offers a useful account of Plato's 'receptacle'. For a rich source of Classical Arabic accounts of material substance see Jon McGinnis and David Reisman (eds), *Classical Arabic Philosophy: An Anthology of Sources* (Hackett 2007). Ted Schmaltz, *Descartes on Causation* (Oxford University Press 2008), chapter 1, gives a useful overview of the broader Classical Arabic, scholastic and early modern context of what I call 'theological materialism'.

For Berkeley's views on the limits of intelligibility and its relation to immaterialism see Stefan Storrie, "The scope of Berkeley's idealism in Berkeley's 1734 edition of the *Three Dialogues*" in Stefan Storrie (ed.), *Berkeley's Three Dialogues: New Essays* (Oxford University Press 2018).

7

A WORLD IN FLUX?

No identity other than perfect likeness in any individuals besides persons.

Notebooks §192

In the first two dialogues Philonous has relentlessly attacked Hylas' belief in material substance. Hylas has given up that notion but he still thinks that material substance is necessary to uphold the reality of sensible things. Therefore, he believes that he does not know anything about the real nature of anything in the world:

> *H:* Material substance was no more than a hypothesis, and a false and groundless one too. I will no longer spend my breath in defence of it. But whatever hypothesis you advance, or whatsoever scheme of things you introduce in its stead, I doubt not it will appear every whit as false; let me but be allowed to question you upon it. That is, suffer me to serve you in your own kind, and I warrant it shall conduct you, through as many perplexities and contradictions, to the very same state of scepticism that I myself am in at present. (229)

The central concern of the third dialogue is to show that Philonous' immaterialism does not succumb to scepticism. It is therefore fitting that Hylas becomes the questioner and the attention turns from a theory of material substance to the coherence of Philonous' immaterialism. Philonous' defence of his position is conducted on two tiers. On one level, as we saw in Chapter 5, he has an account of the metaphysical structure of the world that, he believes, is inferable from the structure of experience. This account puts God at the centre as the sole cause of the existence and intelligibility of most events in the universe. The second tier of Philonous' account was glimpsed at the end of Chapter 6 when he explained how he understood the reality of an everyday sensible object. This is characterized as a common sense account and it is couched in terms of the pragmatics of language and human practices. Philonous references these two aspects of his reply early in the third dialogue in a rhetorical response to Hylas' statement above. "What a jest it is for a philosopher to question the experience of sensible things, till he has it proved to him from the veracity of God; or to pretend our knowledge in this point falls short of intuition and demonstration" (230). This is a reference, first to Descartes' procedure of establishing the existence of the external world by proving that God's reliability underpins the legitimacy of our cognitive faculties in *Meditations* VI, and second to Locke's claim that our knowledge of the existence of external objects is not as great as our knowledge about the relation of ideas such as mathematical knowledge in *Essay* 4.11.3. The challenge for Philonous is to show the overall coherence and connection between these two layers of explanation.

COMMON SENSE AND IMMATERIALISM

In the first dialogue, our two protagonists discussed how different things look in microscopes. Their focus there was on colour. Hylas now returns to this example in an attempt to question Philonous' claim that immaterialism adheres to the common sense precept that the reality of a thing consists in our experience of it:

> H: You say you believe your senses; and seem to applaud yourself that in this you agree with the vulgar. According to you, therefore, the true nature of a thing is discovered by the senses. If so, whence comes that disagreement? Why is not the same figure,

> and other sensible qualities, perceived all manner of ways? And
> why should we use a microscope, the better to discover the true
> nature of a body, if it were discoverable to the naked eye? (245)

They have, Hylas believes, agreed in the first dialogue that the same
thing, say a vial of blood, appears to have different (if any) colour in
different situations. Similarly, if I look at a knife with the naked eye
the edge looks sharp and smooth, but if I look at it in a microscope
it looks jagged. Hylas want to use this feature of our experience to
serve back the problem of a criterion of truth to Philonous. If the reality of a thing is identified with our experience of that thing, but the
experience of the thing differs in different observational situations,
then either the object is radically different in different situations or
we decide that one perceptual situation has priority. If we go for the
former approach, then we have no criterion of veridical experience.
If we go for the latter option, then it would be reasonable to privilege
the perception through the microscope, and declare it to be the truer
perception, just as they did in the first dialogue. In that case, it is not
correct to state that my unaided perception of, say, a glove shows me
the true nature of it, rather, in truth, the glove has a radically different colour, shape, and so on, than that which I come to perceive in
ordinary experience. In this way Hylas hopes to snare Philonous in a
dilemma where both paths lead to scepticism.

Philonous' reply is remarkable and is bound to surprise Hylas:

P: Strictly speaking, Hylas, we do not see the same object that we
    feel; neither is the same object perceived by the microscope,
    which was by the naked eye. But in case every variation was
    thought sufficient to constitute a new kind or individual, the
    endless number or confusion of names would render language
    impracticable. Therefore to avoid this as well as other inconven-
    iences which are obvious upon a little thought, men combine
    together several ideas, apprehended by divers senses, or by the
    same sense at different times or in different circumstances, but
    observed however to have some connection in nature, either
    with respect to co-existence or succession; all which they refer
    to one name and consider as one thing. Hence it follows that
    when I examine by my other senses a thing I have seen, it is
    not in order to understand better the same object which I had

perceived by sight, the object of one sense not being perceived by the other senses. And when I look through a microscope, it is not that I may perceive more clearly what I perceived already with my bare eyes, the object perceived by the glass being quite different from the former. But in both cases my aim is only to know what ideas are connected together; and the more a man knows of the connection of ideas, the more he is said to know of the nature of things. (245)

Philonous makes a number of points in this reply. First, a point about the nature of the sensible. Just as the objects of sight are different from the objects of tactile sensations (the heterogeneity of the sense modalities that Berkeley argues for in the *New Theory*), so too are the objects that we see with the naked eye different from what we see in the microscope. This response would surprise Hylas because it goes against what Hylas had taken himself to be agreeing with Philonous about in the first dialogue when they discussed the criterion of true colour, there they had assumed that it is the same thing that is seen through a microscope and with the naked eye. Second, a point about how language works. The claim here is that language is not designed to track every change in experience. If this were true, there would be far too many words, and we would have to be constantly alert to changes in our perceptual circumstances, or in changes in the objects perceived. Instead language functions by generalizing experience into manageable chunks. The third point is about knowledge. Philonous' claim here is that knowledge is not so much about the perception of ideas as it is about the connection between different ideas. Ideas are connected in various ways in nature according to certain law-like patterns and it is up to us to find good ways of tracking these connections when we devise the concepts that divide up experience into manageable chunks. Philonous' challenge is to make a compelling case for this connection between the changing nature of the sensible and his account of language and knowledge.

SENSIBLE THINGS AND THE PRAGMATICS OF LANGUAGE: A SHORT STORY

To see how Philonous is thinking about the nature of language it is useful to consider Argentinian author Jorge Louis Borges' wonderful short story "Funes the memorious". Borges was well versed in Berkeley's philosophy and was interested in expressing immaterialism and the limits of empiricism through his short stories and essays, including "Tlön, Uqbar, Orbis Tertius" and "A new refutation of time". In "Funes", Borges tells the story of his meeting Ireneo Funes who has had a bad fall and is now disabled. It is revealed that as a consequence of his accident Funes has been rewarded, or cursed, with perfect memory. The world that Funes inhabits by means of this heightened faculty is one of an extraordinarily complex series of discrete sensations where, to use Philonous' expression from the text above "every variation was thought sufficient to constitute a new kind or individual". As Borges explains:

> We, at one glance, can perceive three glasses on a table; Funes, all the leaves and tendrils and fruit that make up a grape vine. He knew by heart the forms of the southern clouds at dawn on the 30th of April, 1882, and could compare them in his memory with the mottled streaks on a book in Spanish binding he had only seen once and with the outlines of the foam raised by an oar in the Rio Negro the night before the Quebracho uprising. These memories were not simple ones; each visual image was linked to muscular sensations, thermal sensations, etc. He could reconstruct all his dreams, all his half-dreams. Two or three times he had reconstructed a whole day; he never hesitated, but each reconstruction had required a whole day. He told me: "I alone have more memories than all mankind has probably had since the world has been the world." And again: "My dreams are like you people's waking hours." And again, toward dawn: "My memory, sir, is like a garbage heap." A circle drawn on a blackboard, a right triangle, a lozenge—all these are forms we can fully and intuitively grasp; Ireneo could do the same with the stormy mane of a pony, with a herd of cattle on a hill, with the changing fire and its innumerable ashes, with the many faces of a dead man throughout a long wake. I don't know how many stars he could see in the sky.

> (1970: 72–3)

There are some people who have capacity for memory that is similar to that described by Borges here, the cases of Solomon Shereshevsky (whom Tom Verberne (1976) has speculated was a real-life inspiration for the fictional Funes) and Jill Price being the most famous. Borges himself also had a phenomenal memory, something that he worked to strengthen through his life as he knew a congenital disease would eventually leave him blind (he lost his sight in 1955, the year he was appointed director of the Argentinian national library). But in Borges' fantasy the awareness of the changing nature of the sensible is greatly enhanced, compared to how most people experience events. Human beings do not normally have the capacity to remember everything we sense, nor do we have the focus of attention to consider all the details of what we experience. Yet this exaggeration gives us a concrete example of what is at stake in Philonous' reply to Hylas' objection. What we actually perceive is much more detailed and complex than we describe it to be, not only to others but also to ourselves. It is sufficient to consider the multitude of different shades of colours that we categorize under that same word, or the innumerable nameless shapes we perceive daily. Philonous', and Borges', point is that experience and language do not map neatly on to one another. As Borges puts it later in "Funes":

> Locke, in the seventeenth century, postulated (and rejected) an impossible language in which each individual thing, each stone, each bird and each branch, would have its own name; Funes once projected an analogous language, but discarded it because it seemed too general to him, too ambiguous. In fact, Funes remembered not only every leaf of every tree of every wood, but also every one of the times he had perceived or imagined it. He decided to reduce each of his past days to some seventy thousand memories, which would then be defined by means of ciphers. He was dissuaded from this by two considerations: his awareness that the task was interminable, his awareness that it was useless. He thought that by the hour of his death he would not even have finished classifying all the memories of his childhood.
>
> (1970: 74)

Locke stated that a language that has a name for each object, as would be expected if language tracks every perceptible unit of experience in the sensible world, would be impractical, for there would be too many words to keep track of (*Essay* 2.11.9). We looked at this issue in some detail in Chapter 4, and found that Locke appeals to abstraction to explain how we generalize the content of experience to linguistically manageable units.

In contrast, Funes, and also Philonous, hold that Locke's imaginary language is in fact too *general* to track perception because it does not take time into consideration. According to Funes and Philonous, things look different in some respect every time they are perceived, and so a language that tracks our perceptions would have to have words for each unity that is sensibly perceived at every moment in time. Luckily, this is not how language works; here Philonous offers an account of language that Funes has problems comprehending. It is not specific perceptions that are units of language. Instead, taking precisely the point about objects being in time into consideration, it is the connection between particular perceptions, the laws that govern change, that we aim at when speaking and when we try to understand or act in the world.

Philonous paints the picture of a world in flux. Hylas believes that this view has consequences that are far from common sense and that are not commensurate with basic shared metaphysical assumptions. He presents two main objections, the identity objection and the continuity objection.

THE IDENTITY OBJECTION

Here is how Hylas introduces the issue:

H: Is it not your opinion that by our senses we perceive only the ideas existing in our minds?

P: It is.

H: But the same idea which is in my mind, cannot be in yours, or in any other mind. Doth it therefore follow from your principles, that no two can see the same thing? And is not this highly absurd? (247)

Since I cannot occupy the same position in space and therefore the same vantage point as another person, I do not, strictly speaking, see the same thing as any other person. Neither do I have the same previous experiences and background assumptions as anyone else when I perceive something Or, similarly, if my attention was as good as Funes', I would be able to differentiate between the thing I see at one moment and the thing I see the next, because I would change my position slightly, or the light would change almost imperceptibly, or the object would undergo some minute change (in the story, Funes is constantly surprised by the way his hands look every time he looks at them because he thinks they have changed so much between every time of seeing them).

Of course, as a matter of fact our attention is (most probably) not as good as Funes' and Hylas therefore rightly focuses on the more obvious apparent absurdity, that different people do not perceive the same thing. Now these questions prompt Philonous to launch into what might be the longest monologue in the whole work, so we will divide it into manageable chunks.

[1] If the term *same* be taken in the vulgar acceptation, it is certain (and not at all repugnant to the principles I maintain) that different persons may perceive the same thing; or the same thing or idea exist in different minds. Words are of arbitrary imposition; and since men are used to apply the word *same* where no distinction or variety is perceived, and I do not pretend to alter their perceptions, it follows, that as men have said before, *several saw the same thing*, so they may upon like occasions still continue to use the same phrase, without any deviation either from the propriety of language, or the truth of things.

(247)

Here Philonous is saying that the word 'same' means "no distinction or variety is perceived". The point is then that people see pretty similar things and this is enough to call them the same. But how much similarity is enough? On one view "no distinction or variety is perceived" means 'agree sufficiently' and that the lack of distinction or variety is not a fact about the world but is something that is reached by a process of consensus.

Take, for example, this table in front of me. It is a fairly big, oval, brown thing in my living room, and it is the only such object in this room. My friends who will visit this evening will all perceive the thing that corresponds to this description when they are roughly in the same place as I. Someone who possesses a greater colour vocabulary than I might say that it is a chestnut brown or maroon or some other shade that is broadly within the range of the colour that we call 'brown', we might disagree about the exact shade, we might disagree about whether the lighting is ideal but a broad consensus can typically be reached. Since we all agree that we perceive something corresponding to the description, and since there is no doubt about there being other things that fit this description, Philonous can therefore say that we all perceive the same thing. If the description were altered, that would be no problem. If the table had a green leg on my side of it then you could come around and perceive that too. On this reading of "no distinction or variety is perceived" agreement in the description of what is perceived is all there is to sameness. But are things really so simple?

We might wonder how much agreement is sufficient. Even if we have sufficient agreement for all sorts of practical things we might think that it is unsuitable to use the word 'same'. We can certainly distinguish what I perceive from what my friends around the table perceive, even when perceiving this table, and we can do so with the resources of common language. From a different vantage point the table might seem more rectangular, or one might think it is more bole in colour, whereas I insist it has a more chestnut colour. The idea of sameness as agreement about a general description could then be problematic because sameness or identity seems to carry with it an idea of a very strong agreement. There are reasons for concern here, but Philonous has plenty more to say on the subject.

[2] But if the term *same* be used in the acceptation of philosophers, who pretend to an abstract notion of identity, then, according to their sundry definitions of this notion (for it is not yet agreed wherein that philosophical identity consists), it may or may not be possible for diverse persons to perceive the same thing. But whether philosophers shall think fit to call a thing the *same* or no, is, I conceive, of small importance.

(247)

Philonous now says that that 'philosophical identity' is a vague notion about which there is no agreement at all. He is presumably gesturing towards the problem of finding a criterion of individuality, which has vexed philosophers throughout history, and which is sometimes called the search for the *principium individuationis* (principle of individuation). In the early modern period this topic was taken up thematically by Locke in his second edition of the *Essay*. He did this to satisfy a request from William Molyneux. As Locke says in a letter from 23 August 1693, just a few months after Molyneux's request: "you will herewith receive a new chapter Of identity and diversity, which, having writ only at your instance, 'tis fit you should see and judge of it before it goes to the press" (*Corr.* 1655).

Locke confidently states that "'tis easy to discover, what is so much enquired after, the *principium Individuationis*, and that 'tis plain is Existence it self, which determines a Being of any sort to a particular time and place incommunicable to two Beings of the same kind" (*Essay* 2.27.3). The identity criterion is captured by the description of what makes a thing be a thing of a certain kind or sort, such as a "tree". Locke called these kinds of description "sortal" (*Essay* 2.27.3). In contrast, other general adjectival descriptions, such as "green" are not linked to identity conditions because what is described as green might not be an individual object but a part of an object, such as a leaf on a tree, or a part of a leaf. These kinds of descriptions merely give us a criterion for determining those things to which the term is applicable, without identifying the sort of thing it is.

According to Locke, sortal terms are abstract ideas that identify objects because the description allows us to pick out and enumerate individuals of this kind. The identity conditions are different for different kinds of things. Locke argues that the identity condition for inanimate objects or parcels of matter that consists of "two or more Atoms", referred to by 'mass nouns' such as 'wood' or 'sand', is the "Mass, consisting of the same Atoms" (*Essay* 2.27.3). In this way, the identity criterion is connected to one of Locke's primary qualities, which we have not considered yet, namely, number. At one point in the *Essay* Locke states that "number of parts" (*Essay* 4.3.15) is a primary quality that an object has. For these parcels of matter, this corresponds to a finite number equal to the number of 'atoms', which for Locke are indivisible corpuscles. For other classes of things, the identity criterion will look quite different. For example, living organisms go through various developmental phases. A tree starts out as a seed and then grows progressively larger. Therefore, what makes a tree the same tree is not its number of 'atoms' but the fact that it has a number of parts that work together "partaking in one Common Life" (*Essay* 2.27.4). Here a different conception of number as primary quality is at work. This is observed in the *Essay* in the section called "Of number" where Locke says that each thing suggests to us the idea of unity (*Essay* 2.16.1)

While the identity criterion is different for different sortal terms, Locke seems to be of the opinion that the identity criteria are fixed for each sortal category and that objective descriptions of these criteria are achievable. There is one set of criteria that makes an inanimate thing that kind of thing, rather than another, and it is one criterion that makes a particular tree one tree or a particular house one house. Philonous continues his discussion by explaining through an example why he rejects the idea that sortal terms give unique identity conditions:

> P: Or suppose a house, whose walls or outward shell remains unaltered, the chambers are all pulled down, and new ones built in their place; and that you should call this the *same*, and I should say it was not the *same* house: would we not for all this perfectly agree in our thoughts of the house, considered in itself? And would not all the difference consist in a sound? If you should say, we differed in our notions; for that you super-added to your idea of the house the simple abstracted idea of identity, whereas I did not; I would tell you I know not what you mean by abstract idea of identity and should desire you to look into your own thoughts, and be sure you understand yourself. – Why so silent, Hylas? Are you not yet satisfied, men may dispute about identity and diversity, without any real difference in their thoughts and opinions, abstracted from names? (248)

We can illustrate Philonous' point here by considering the following two judgements (1) "H1 and H2 are identical" and (2) "H1 and H2 are not identical". What is the disagreement between the parties who make these judgements about? It is not about anything perceived; for both parties recognize that, in the house in question, there is an interior difference and an exterior sameness. Philonous states that the only difference in the two judgements is a sound, that one utters the word 'same' and the other 'different' or 'not same'. Is this correct? It seems a bit crude; could we not detect some difference in the thoughts expressed in the two judgements? The obvious difference is in the understanding of the concept 'house'. One person might take it to include the interior and exterior of the building while another understands by the same word only the building's exterior. This seems quite plausible, but then what is the difference in the judgement about? Philonous' point is that the difference is in how the term 'house' is understood to apply to one's perception, not the additional understanding of an identity criterion based on the 'being' or (nominal) essence of 'house'. If the conclusion from this example is generalized, as Philonous seems to want it to be, his position is, then, that all sortal terms only have a criterion of applicability and not an additional criterion of identity. As a consequence, all cases of settling the identity of an object are conventional and decided by an arbitrary criterion that is relative to how a group decides to define that object. Sortal terms do not have a further, more objective, component added to them.

At the heart of Locke's idea of an identity criterion is the notion that number is a primary quality. That the number of parts and the unity of each thing is built in to the basic nature of each thing independently of how one conceives of them. Berkeley emphatically rejects this idea because he thinks that number, of all the proposed primary qualities, is the one that is most obviously purely mind-dependent. Since number does not belong to the object, there is no objective identity criterion.

> That number is entirely the creature of the mind, even though the other qualities be allowed to exist without, will be evident to whoever considers, that the same thing bears a different denomination to number, as the mind views it with different respects. Thus, the same extension is one, or three, or thirty six, according as the mind considers it with reference to a yard, a foot, or an inch. Number is so visibly relative, and depends on men's understanding, that it is strange to think how any one should give it an absolute existence without the mind. We say one book, one page, one line; all these are equally units, though some contain several of the others. And in each instance it is plain, the unit relates to some particular combination of ideas arbitrarily put together by the mind.

> (*Principles* §12)

In the next part of Philonous' monologue he poses the question he is trying to answer on behalf of immaterialism to Hylas. How does materialism deal with identity? If it fares no better or no worse than immaterialism, then can the problem of identity be an objection to one or the other of the theories? Philonous and Hylas would think not since they agree on the principle that "that which makes equally against two contradictory positions, can be proof against neither" (248).

> P: Take this farther reflexion with you: that whether matter be allowed to exist or no, the case is exactly the same as to the point at hand. For the materialist themselves acknowledge what we immediately perceive by our senses, to be our own idea. Your difficulty therefore, that no two see the same thing, makes equally against the materialists and me. (248)

If the materialist accepts, as Hylas did at the end of the first dialogue, that we immediately perceive by sense only ideas, then he would also accept that no two persons have the same idea. Therefore, Philonous thinks, the same problem arises for the materialist. But of course no materialist would accept this. Because while they have different ideas, the ideas are caused by or resemble or are about the same thing, the material house, for example. On the materialist hypothesis, the fact that we have different ideas does not mean that the things themselves are different. Hylas, unsurprisingly, says, "But they [the materialists] suppose an external archetype, to which referring their several ideas, they may truly be said to perceive the same thing" (248).

What can Philonous reply to this? He could refer back to the last two days of discussion, especially the end of the second dialogue, where they agreed that matter cannot be the cause or occasion of ideas, or an instrument for the creation of ideas, indeed that the very idea of matter playing such a role is either contradictory or meaningless. Philonous does make this point, but also reminds Hylas that on the immaterialist account there is also room for such archetypes.

> P: And (not to mention your having discarded those archetypes) so may you suppose an external archetype on my principles; *external*, I mean, to your own mind though indeed it must be supposed to exist in that mind which comprehends all things; but then this serves all the ends of identity, as well as if it existed out of a mind. And I am sure you will not say, it is less intelligible. (248)

Having argued at length that the metaphysical notion of identity is meaningless Philonous now goes ahead and actually offers a metaphysical conception of identity based on his immaterialist principles. He is saying that if you really press me on the commonality that allows us to use the same words for our different ideas, then I can, if I must, refer to the ideas that God has of the things he creates. They are like the ideas a craftsman has of for example a chair, while he is making it, and are, therefore, analogous to blueprints. Can there be one such archetype for each thing that we call the same? Does not every idea I have require a separate archetype from each idea that you have? Because otherwise, how are we to account for the difference? To approach these questions it is instructive to note that Berkeley often uses the idea that God is literally the author of nature. He speaks directly to each one of us, but not separately to each one of us. A public speaker says one thing, but the same story (archetypes) is understood in slightly different ways by the hearers, they have slightly different ideas on the basis of the words that they hear in different ways. So the difference in the ideas comes from our individual situation.

We have seen that Hylas raises the identity problem to attempt to show that the conception of reality that follows from immaterialism is one of constant flux in a very strong sense, that no two people perceive the same thing. Philonous answer to this is rather complex. He has a two-tiered defence. One is at the level of experience and common sense, the other is at a highly abstract metaphysical and theological level.

Immaterialism:	idea – archetype (idea)
Materialism:	idea – archetype (matter)
	Challenge of having a coherent conception of archetype.
Where is the identity in the changing ideas themselves?	

If we speak of the identity and diversity of sensible things, then yes, strictly speaking ideas are different for each person. But our limited minds do not register the flux, rather we have permanence, or at least stability due to the human limitations of attention and memory.

Further, the nature of language is such that it simplifies reality and lets us generalize according to rules of convention. In fact, these two points are closely connected. I can't remember the details of a table that I perceived in a friend's house a month ago, but I do remember that it was a big oak table. The concepts 'table', 'oak' and 'big' help me *both* to remember and communicate things, though they are general words and do not perfectly accurately reflect my particular experience of the table at the time. If we understand our own limitations and if we understand the way language works, it is not surprising that we can call things perceived at different times or by different people *the same* and that we are justified in doing so.

On a different level, Philonous also denies that when one person perceives an object it is not even strictly speaking different from the object that another person perceives. This is because the sensible world is grounded on God's ideas of how the world should be. God creates sensible ideas in us on the basis of his ideas, and so things, or ideas, have a cause that serves all the purposes of identity on Philonous' conception of metaphysical reality. Philonous' arguments in the second dialogue also serve to undermine a materialist alternative to identity at this level.

THE CONTINUITY OBJECTION

Since Philonous holds that the being of sensible things exists in their being perceived, it follows that sensible things do not exist when they are not perceived. When I am in my living room, I do not perceive my kitchen. Do the sensible things that make up my kitchen cease to exist when I am in my living room? In general, do sensible things continually pop into and out of existence as they are perceived or not perceived by various finite minds? Like the identity objection, this raises issues central to the immaterialist doctrine and it is a question on which Philonous, and Berkeley in his other writings, is sometimes guarded and ambivalent and sometimes daring in his pronouncements.

Hylas raises the issue in the following way:

> H: Supposing you were annihilated, cannot you conceive it possible, that things perceivable by sense may still exist. (230)

Hylas' point appears to be that if I cannot conceive it possible to perceive something then it cannot exist. But I cannot conceive things after I am dead, just as I could not before I was born. But it is absurd to think that things didn't exist before my birth and will cease to exist after my death. Therefore things must exist regardless of whether I can possibly conceive them or not. Philonous replies as follows:

> P: I can; but then it must be in another mind. When I deny sensible things an existence out of the mind, I do not mean my mind in particular, but all minds. Now it is plain they have an existence exterior to my mind, since I find them by experience to be independent of it. There is therefore some other mind wherein they exist, during the intervals between the times of my perceiving them: as likewise they did before my birth, and would do after my supposed annihilation. (230–1)

As long as some mind perceives, there is a world. So the answer to Hylas' challenge lies in other minds perceiving. In the *Principles*, however, Berkeley gives another solution, which is somewhat weaker, or, at least, more minimal, it proves only what is necessary to answer the objection.

> If we consider it, the objection proposed in Section 45 [things are constantly annihilated and created anew according to immaterialism] will not be found reasonable charged on the principles we have premised, so as in truth to make any objection at all against our notions. For though we hold indeed the objects of sense to be nothing but ideas which cannot exist unperceived; yet we may not hence conclude they have no existence except only while they are perceived by us, since there may be some other spirit that perceives them, though we do not.
>
> (*Principles* §48)

This seems like a weak reply because it invokes scepticism to answer the objection. Berkeley is saying here that we cannot be absolutely sure that things are annihilated all the time, because it is possible that some other mind perceives the thing. Since Berkeley and Philonous claim to not be sceptical at all it seems disingenuous to invoke scepticism here.

There is, however, another way that we can look at this. Berkeley seems to say that there is something wrong with the objection itself, which parallels his commonsensical approach to the identity objection. In that case he says that the problem should not arise at all because it is wrong to look for metaphysical identity in the realm of ideas. In the realm of experience perception and knowledge are intimately linked. From the fact that we do not perceive an object, it follows that we do not know what is going on with it and around it. By diverting our attention away from an object there will be a level of uncertainty and indeterminacy. Strictly speaking we do not know if an object that no one perceives continues to exist, because existence is something that is verified by experience, which is why we cannot prove that something exists by logic alone. In the realm of experience, it is true for immaterialists and materialists alike that we know things to exist by experiencing them. Therefore the problem of continuity is not specific to immaterialism, but is shared also by the materialists. The burden of answering the question of whether a thing has ceased to exist when no one is perceiving it is does not fall solely on the shoulders of those who affirm that the existence of things consists in their being perceived. For even if its existence depends on material substance it could be the case that the material substance itself ceases to exist when unperceived (since the only way we can know that the material substance is present is through the presence of the sensible thing that they supposedly cause). In summary, Berkeley's point is this. I can know that a thing exists in two ways: either I perceive the thing myself, or someone else perceives it. But if no one perceives the thing in question, then I cannot know that it exists. This is the case both for materialists and immaterialists. And that which counts equally against two contradictory views is not proof against either. So strict continuity, in the sense of a continuous awareness of the existence of sensible things is not something we should expect on any understanding of what underlies sensible things.

This cannot be the whole story, however. As we saw in Chapter 5, Philonous' move from the statement that a spirit wills and understand all sensible things in the universe to the claim that this spirit is the Christian God, requires that sensible things exist continuously. Philonous does not give the reader much of an argument for this claim. As we have seen in this section, when discussing continuity explicitly Philonous is not presenting an argument for the claim that sensible things do exist continuously, but only for the claim that they may exist in such a way. In Chapter 5 I presented Rickless' (2018) suggestion that Philonous is basing his belief in the continued existence of sensible things on an argument from best explanation, according to which the explanans is the apparent stability of the sensible world. I think it is questionable that this is the best explanation. The stability and predictability of the sensible world are equally well explained on the assumption that God creates and destroys sensible things in accordance with whether anyone is perceiving them or not. We can see this if we consider the example of someone watching a film on a screen with a sensor connected to her eyes such that the screen will go blank when she looks away, and when the person looks back at the screen, the film switches on again, continuing as *if* it has been running in the background. The film, I submit, will be just as coherent to the viewer in that situation as it would be if, *in fact*, it kept running in the background when she was not watching. Why? Because in both cases, whenever the viewer looks at the screen she sees the unfolding of the story as it is supposed to be, that is, as coherent and stable as it can be. Perhaps all Philonous means by continuity is that God keeps track of all the things that are going on such that when someone is there to perceive something the correct ideas will be presented. Sensible things are then in God's mind continuously but they are in his mind merely as archetypes and not as sensible things.

This approach appears to be confirmed towards the end of the *Three Dialogues*, when the interlocutors consider whether immaterialism is compatible with the Mosaic story of creation. This discussion was prompted by an objection raised by Catherine Percival, the wife of Berkeley's old friend Sir John Percival. In a letter 26 August 1710 John says: "My wife [. . .] desires to know if there be nothing but spirit and ideas, what you make of that part of the six days' creation which preceded man."

> H: What shall we make then of the Creation?
> P: May we not understand it to have been entirely in respect of finite spirits; so that things, with regard to us, may properly be said to begin their existence, or be created, when God decreed they should become perceptible to intelligent creatures, in that order and manner which he then established, and we now call the laws of Nature? You may call this a *relative* or *hypothetical* existence if you please. [. . .]

P: What would you have! do I not acknowledge a twofold state of things, the one ectypal or natural, the other archetypal and eternal? The former was created in time; the latter from everlasting in the mind of God. (253–4)

God has had the idea of the sun and moon for all eternity in the "divine intellect" (253). What happens in creation is that God decides that things will become perceptible to finite minds. Here Philonous' point is that the real existence of the natural world is the sensible world which is dependent on finite perceivers and so is the "relative" or "ectypal" state of things. What is perceived and known is real, what is absolute and eternal is mere possibility. On this view we can make sense of Philonous' claim that "I am not for changing things into ideas, but rather ideas into things; since those immediate objects of perception, which according to you are only appearances of things, I take to be the real things themselves" (244).

FURTHER READING

The extraordinary memory of Solomon Shereshevsky is documented in A. R. Luria, *The Mind of a Mnemonist: A Little Book about a Vast Memory* (Harvard University Press 1987). Many of Borges' short stories are collected in Jorge Borges' *Labyrinths* (Penguin 2000). A useful account of Locke's views on identity is Jonathan Lowe, *The Routledge Philosophy Guidebook to Locke on Human Understanding* (Routledge 1995), chapter 5.

Berkeley's approach to the continuity and identity objection is considered in detail by Kenneth Winkler, *Berkeley: An Interpretation* (Clarendon Press 1989), chapter 7; Tom Stoneham, *Berkeley's World* (Oxford University Press 2002), chapters 5 and 8; and Seth Bordner, "If we stop thinking about Berkeley's problem of continuity, will it still exist?" *Journal of the History of Philosophy*, 55 (2): 237–60.

8

MIND AND MORALITY

It seems improper & liable to difficulties to make the Word Person stand for an Idea, or to make ourselves ideas or thinking things ideas.

Notebooks §523

The two great principles of morality. the Being of God and the Freedom of Man: these to be handled in the beginning of the Second Book.

Notebooks §508

Berkeley aimed to significantly expand his discussion of mind and morality in his projected Part II of the *Principles*. He was planning for the contents of this book already in his *Notebooks* (§§508, 878). He was working on this manuscript while on his Italian sojourn in 1716–21, but, and this ranks as one of the great tragedies in the history of philosophy, he lost the manuscript on his travels and decided not to start over again. We are therefore in a peculiar situation with regard to the content of Berkeley's philosophy. By rejecting material substance and by arguing that sensible things are mind-dependent, the mind becomes the central component of his philosophy. Yet the nature of the mind is not a topic that Berkeley treats in an exhaustive way in the *Principles* or the *Three Dialogues*. Likewise, the purpose of Berkeley's philosophy is to lead mankind away from error, to see things aright and as a consequence to be able to think and act for the good of mankind and oneself. As he explains in the Preface to the *Three Dialogues* "the end of speculation [is] practice, or the improvement of our lives and actions" (167). Yet there is no moral theory presented in either the *Principles* or the *Three Dialogues*.

Instead of rewriting Part II of the *Principles* Berkeley engaged in discussions of the nature of mind and morality in some of his later works such as *Alciphron* and *Siris*. He also added new sections to the *Principles* and the *Three Dialogues* in the 1734 editions of those works, which do add to our understanding of his conception of the mind. Finally, Berkeley had already in 1712 written *Passive Obedience*, which is a brief work on the Tory and Anglican doctrine of duty to the sovereign and which includes an outline of a broader moral theory; in particular, it outlines a theory of moral obligation. In this chapter I will, accordingly draw on a larger range of texts to explain some of the central topics of Berkeley's philosophy of mind and moral philosophy, taking the *Three Dialogues* as a starting point.

SELF-KNOWLEDGE

Berkeley seems to follow his early modern predecessors in his conception of the nature of the mind. In accordance with Descartes he takes the mind to essentially be a thinking substance. A crucial difference is that Philonous' immaterialism takes mind to be the only substance. Yet, in the first two dialogues the focus is not directly on minds but on sensible things understood as ideas and the dependence relation that obtains between those things and the mind. We saw in the discussion of the act–object theory in Chapter 4 that Philonous holds that a crucial feature of the mind, which sets it apart from an idea, is that it is active. We saw in the discussion of God as an infinite mind in Chapter 5 that Philonous assigns all causal powers to minds. This suggests, as Berman (1994) has pointed out, that there is a basic duality in the world between minds and ideas. This is not a duality of substances, for mind is the only substance, but a duality between mind as that which fundamentally exists as activity and as cause, and ideas as the inert things that the mind creates. On this model, finite minds such as human beings, possible other intelligences, and God are what constitute fundamental reality.

We have seen that, in the third dialogue, Philonous' immaterialism comes under scrutiny. Berkeley's choice to discuss the mind explicitly only in the third dialogue shows that he is concerned with addressing certain objections that could be raised against the immaterialist position. As James Hill (2018) has shown, the fundamental issue that concerns Hylas and Philonous' discussion of the mind in the third dialogue is the problem of understanding self-knowledge as perception. Berkeley's predecessors took knowledge of the self to consist in a form of inward perception. In *Meditations* III Descartes describes the activity involved in the "faculty by which I perceive myself" in terms of "when I turn the mind's eye toward myself" (CMS II 51) Likewise, Locke took the mind to be able not only to perceive outward ideas through sensation but also to form ideas of the mind's operations through a perceptive act that he calls "reflecion" (*Essay* 2.1.4). If one accepts the idea that self-knowledge requires perception of a kind of idea, this can lead to scepticism about knowledge of the self, if one also believes that there is no idea to be found by turning one's eye toward oneself. For example, Hobbes objected to Descartes' view that when a person experiences fear (for example, when being charged by a lion), she perceives herself as having this fear. Hobbes instead holds that what this person perceives when she feels the fear is not *herself* feeling fear, but the *thing* that she fears and, as an effect of this, the strong inclination to take flight (AT VII 182). If these kinds of episodes reveal that no idea of the self is present in internal perceptions, then we might wonder if we really have any knowledge of the self. Indeed, Hobbes' conclusion is that we do not: "the soul is something of which we have no idea at all" (AT VII 183). For all this, Hobbes did not reject the perceptual model. Instead of inward perception, he sought to ground our awareness of the self in perceptions of our body (AT VII 180).

In the third dialogue Philonous agrees with Hobbes that an examination of our internal activities would not reveal any idea of ourselves. He does not appeal to introspection to determine this, but instead takes it to be a consequence of the aforementioned duality between mind and idea. The suggestion is that as minds are essentially active they, or their specific activities such as willing, loving, or fearing, cannot be represented by essentially passive ideas. As Flage (2014: 125) has pointed out, this is a valid inference if the only kind of representation possible in this case is one of resemblance. Perhaps there are other ways of thinking about representation in this context; however, it is not something that Berkeley considers in the *Three Dialogues*.

Hylas picks up on the incompatibility between the perceptual model of self-knowledge and Philonous' dualism and launches a three-pronged attack: how can Philonous account for our knowledge of (a) our selves, (b) other finite minds, and (c) God's mind? In this section we will consider the first question and in the next section we will consider the other two issues. When Hylas queries Philonous about these three issues he is at the same time attempting to resurrect his belief in matter. He does so by arguing that there is parity between our knowledge of the mind and our knowledge of matter. His thought here is that if Philonous believes that mind exists even though it cannot be perceived, why deny that material substance exists on the grounds that it is not perceived?

> *H:* [Y]ou acknowledge you have, properly speaking, no idea of your own soul. You even affirm that spirits are a sort of beings altogether different from ideas; consequently that no idea can be like a spirit. We have therefore no idea of any spirit. You admit nevertheless that there is spiritual substance, although you have no idea of it; while you deny there can be such a thing as material substance, because you have no notion or idea of it. Is this fair dealing? To act consistently, you must either admit matter or reject spirit. What say you to this? (232)

Philonous explains that his problem with material substance is much deeper than a mere inability to perceive it. As we saw in Chapter 6 Philonous thinks that the notion of material substance as cause, instrument or occasion for ideas is conceptually incoherent, and that the notion of matter as something that upholds reality is empty and therefore meaningless. Though he agrees with Hylas' assessment that we can have no idea of minds "for these being active, cannot be represented by things perfectly inert, as our ideas are", he does not think this precludes knowledge of the self:

> "I do nevertheless know that I, who am a spirit or thinking substance, exist as certainly as I know my ideas exist. Farther, I know what I mean by the terms 'I' and 'myself'; and I know this immediately, or intuitively, though I do not perceive it as I perceive a triangle, a colour, or a sound" (231)

How do we know ourselves if it is not through forming ideas of ourselves? Philonous does not give much detail. What he does say is that our self-knowledge is "immediate", "intuitive", and a little bit later, that it is acquired by a "reflex act" (232). Clearly, by 'reflex act' he cannot mean what Locke means by 'refection', since the latter is the formation of an (internal) idea. Flage (2014: 127) has noted that Philonous (and indeed Berkeley in various other writings) uses 'reflection' as synonymous with 'reasoning'. Now, reasoning as opposed to sensing, is explicitly *not* the topic of the *Three Dialogues*. In the beginning of the first dialogue, when they are deciding on the conditions for their competition to be the least sceptical, Hylas states that it will involve affirming the truth and reality of things. Philonous immediately clarifies that by 'things' they will be referring to 'sensible things', as opposed to "universal intellectual notions" (173). Nevertheless, it is possible to get some indication of what self-knowledge is on the basis of an adjacent passage that Berkeley inserted into the third (1734) edition of the *Three Dialogues*.

> P: How often must I repeat, that I know or am conscious of my own being; and that I know that I myself am not my ideas, but somewhat else, a thinking active principle that perceives, knows, wills, and operates about ideas. I know that I, one and the same self, perceive both colours and sounds: that a colour cannot perceive a sound, nor a sound a colour: that I am therefore one individual principle, distinct from colour and sound; and, for the same reason, from all other sensible things and inert ideas. (234–5)

One suggestion (Hill 2018: 121ff) is that Berkeley is here stating that self-awareness consists in awareness or consciousness of the unity of perception. According to Philonous, ideas are disparate and are only unified through an act of mind, as we saw in the discussion of identity. This is also a point Berkeley explored in more detail in *Siris*, where he states: "The mind, by virtue of her simplicity, conferreth simplicity upon compounded beings" (356). Of course, we get to know that our experience is unified by the mind indirectly, through numerous steps of reasoning. For example, by analysing the concept of identity as applied to sensible things, as Philonous does in the third dialogue. Or by discovering the heterogeneity of sense modalities as Berkeley does in the *New Theory*. Or by supporting the hypothesis that disparate sensible features are 'glued together' into sensible objects through a series of empirical experiments undertaken in cognitive psychology by, for example, Anne Treisman and her associates (Treisman & Gelade 1980; Treisman & Schmidt 1982). But that experience is a unity, is not something that we arrive at by any number of inferences or other forms of reasoning. Instead, it is the datum that the aforementioned investigations aim to explain in the first place. On the suggestion we are considering, it is this awareness of the unity of experience that is known immediately. Further, it is not knowledge through ideas, we do not perceive this unity of experience as we perceive a sensible thing, but rather it is the awareness that all ideas are organized together in a certain way.

KNOWLEDGE OF OTHER MINDS

Philonous accordingly allows that we know our own selves in a way entirely different from ideas, and he holds that such knowledge is immediate and intuitive. It seems that this approach is not available in explaining our knowledge of other minds because while our own awareness of ourselves can be construed as immediate, our knowledge of other minds seems to require that we project intelligence into those portions of experience we call 'other people', and that seems to require a process, such as an inference, that is not direct. Further, because such awareness is indirect, it seems that the knowledge we gain would be a kind of representation of the other mind, and Philonous has not given us any alternative representation other than ideas. Hylas begins his questioning about this issue with reference to God:

H: Since therefore you have no idea of the mind of God, how can you conceive it possible that things should exist in his mind? [. . .]

P: However, taking the word 'idea' in a large sense, my soul may be said to furnish me with an idea, that is, an image or likeness of God, though indeed extremely inadequate. For all the notion I have of God is obtained by reflecting on my own soul, heightening its powers, and removing its imperfections. I have therefore, though not an inactive idea, yet in myself some sort of an active thinking image of the Deity. And though I perceive him not by sense, yet I have a notion of Him or know Him by reflection and reasoning. My own mind and my own ideas I have an immediate knowledge of; and by the help of these, do mediately apprehend the possibility of the existence of other spirits and ideas. (231–2)

Philonous is quite clear that he takes our knowledge of God to be mediate. At the ground level we have the immediate, non-idea awareness of ourselves that we grappled with in the previous section. Philonous thinks that we can build on that awareness, by first conceiving of ourselves and then heightening our powers, and by removing all those imperfections we see in ourselves. We then form what Philonous calls a 'notion' of God. Prior to the 1734 editions of his works Berkeley used the term 'notion' as broadly synonymous with 'idea'. In the 1734 editions he changes his position and states that the term 'notion' is a technical term that specifies a kind of non-sensible, 'intellectual' knowledge. It is specifically meant to designate the non-idea kind of knowledge or awareness that we have of active minds. As he puts it in the *Principles*: "We may not I think strictly be said to have an idea of an active being, or of an action, although we may be said to have a notion of them. I have some knowledge or notion of my mind, and its acts about ideas, inasmuch as I know or understand what is meant by those words" (§142, 1734 edition only). As Winkler (1989: 279–80n2) explains, Berkeley's usage of the term in 1734 is in line with Ralph Cudworth's usage in the *True Intellectual System* (1837 [1678]: 636) where he contrasts "*Sensible Ideas*" with "*Intelligible Notions*".

As with our own selves, we do not know of the existence of God through experience but through reason. As we saw in Chapter 5, we infer the existence of God on the basis of observations about the sensible world, such as our lack of power with regard to what sensible thing we are to perceive, and the orderly structure of the universe. The case is different with other finite minds. To put it crudely, other finite minds need not exist for me and the world to exist. So the existence of other minds is not inferred through examining the structure of experience but discovered indirectly through experience. In Philonous' words: "It is granted we have neither an immediate evidence nor a demonstrative knowledge of the existence of other finite spirits" (233). Instead it is merely probable that other finite minds exist because "we see signs and effects indicating distinct finite agents like our selves" (233). In the *Three Dialogues*, Philonous does not expand on what the relevant signs and effects are. In the fourth dialogue of *Alciphron* Berkeley expanded significantly on this issue. In this dialogue Euphranor is advocating Berkeley's position and Alciphron is his opponent. Alciphron starts out with a position that can be described as 'Hobbesian', he believes that the relevant signs and effects are bodily motion. By section 6 Euphranor has brought him over to a different view:

> A: Upon this point, I have found that nothing so much convinces me of the existence of another person as his speaking to me. It is my hearing you talk that, in strict philosophical truth, is to me the best argument for your being. (*Alciphron* 4.6)

Alciphron expresses the view that perceiving the use of language is the surest sign of the existence of other people. This has been a common view in the history of thought, held explicitly by Descartes in his 1637 work *Discourse on Method* (AT VI 56, CSM I, 139–40) and relied on more recently by Alan Turing (1950) in the famous 'Turing test' which is an important concept in contemporary AI studies. More specifically, by using language is meant the ability to combine according to rules, constructed and arbitrary signs and to do so in relation to a background setting and appropriate context.

Berkeley added his *New Theory* to *Alciphron* as an appendix. The reason for this was that the argument just presented for the existence of other finite minds gives Berkeley what he needs to construct a new argument for the existence of God, which finally puts his vision of

God as the Author of nature, first expressed and supported in *New Theory*, into relief. As Euphranor explains, given the heterogeneity of visual and tactile ideas, and given the relationship between these kinds of sensations, it follows that the sensible world, in so far as it is comprised of visual and tactile ideas, is literally a language. Visual sensations are completely different from tactile ideas, yet they, through an arbitrary connection just like grammar in human languages, suggest various tactile ideas to the person who sees, just as words suggest meaning. Alciphron, clearly astonished concludes: "I see, therefore, in strict philosophical truth, that rock only in the same sense that I may be said to hear it, when the word *rock* is pronounced" (*Alciphron* 4.11). It follows from this that if Alciphron accepts that he knows other finite minds from the language they evince, so also must he infer the existence of God from the language of nature. If he denies the latter he must also deny the former. As David Berman has succinctly put it, the choice is between "God and solipsism" (1993: 201).

MORALITY: THE LAWS OF PAIN AND PLEASURE

Towards the end of the *Principles*, Berkeley makes the following remark about our knowledge of God:

> [I]f we attentively consider the constant regularity, order, and concatenation of natural things, the surprising magnificence, beauty, and perfection of the larger, and the exquisite contrivance of the smaller parts of the creation, together with the exact harmony and correspondence of the whole, but above all, the never enough admired laws of pain and pleasure, and the instincts or natural inclinations, appetites, and passion of animals; I say if we consider all these things, and at the same time attend to the meaning and import of the attributes, one, eternal, infinitely wise, good, and perfect, we shall clearly perceive that they belong to the aforesaid spirit, *who works all in all*, and *by whom all things consist*.
>
> (*Principles* 146)

It is noteworthy that what Berkeley singles out here is not the traditional aspects of world-design, those of "surprising magnificence", the "beauty, and perfection of the larger, and the exquisite contrivance of the smaller parts of creation", or the "harmony" and "correspondence" of things in nature. No, instead he states that "above all" the central aspect of the world that shows that God "*works all in all*, and *by whom all things consist*" is "the never enough admired laws of pain and pleasure". The laws of pain and pleasure are God's 'language of nature' just discussed. According to Berkeley the sensible world is a system of signs and signifiers that make up a language. This language consists of visual and tactile ideas. The signifiers, the meaning of the world, are tactile sensations. If Philonous takes the assimilation argument to be applicable to all tactile sensations, then all tactile sensations are really different degrees of pleasure and pain. Reality, at least for beings capable of sensation, that is, all finite beings, is a nexus of pleasure and pain. Why is reality thus arranged? This is explained through Berkeley's moral philosophy.

In the first part of *Passive Obedience* Berkeley makes a number of claims that bear on his conception of moral obligation. I want to begin by looking at four passages that constitute Berkeley's argument for why we have maximally rational prudential reasons to follow God's will:

1. "Self-love being a principle of all others the most universal, and the most deeply engraven in our hearts, it is natural for us to regard things as they are fitted to augment or impair our own happiness; and accordingly we denominate them good or evil. Our judgment is ever employ'd in distinguishing between these two, and it is the whole business of our lives to endeavour, by a proper application of our faculties, to procure the one and avoid the other." (*Passive Obedience* 6: 19)

2. "At our first coming into the world, we are entirely guided by the impressions of sense; sensible pleasure being the infallible characteristic of present good, as pain is of evil. But, by degrees, as we grow up in our acquaintance with the nature of things, experience informs us that present good is afterwards oft attended with a greater evil; and, on the other side, that present evil is not less frequently the occasion of procuring to us a greater future good. Besides, as the nobler faculties of the human soul begin to display themselves, they discover to us goods far more excellent than those which affect the senses. [. . .] This obliges us frequently

to overlook present momentary enjoyments, when they come in competition with greater and more lasting goods, though too far off, or of too refined a nature, to affect our senses." (*Passive Obedience* 6: 19)

3. "But as the whole Earth, and the entire duration of those perishing things contained in it, is altogether inconsiderable, or, in the prophet's expressive style, 'less than nothing' in respect of Eternity, who sees not that every reasonable man ought so to frame his actions as that they may most effectually contribute to promote his eternal interest?" (*Passive Obedience* 6: 20)

4. "And since it is a truth evident by the light of nature, that there is a sovereign omniscient Spirit, who alone can make us for ever happy, or for ever miserable; it plainly follows that a conformity to His will, and not any prospect of temporal advantage, is the sole rule whereby every man who acts up to the principles of reason must govern and square his actions." (*Passive Obedience* 6: 20)

In (1) Berkeley states that self-interest is the "most universal" principle of action. He then continues by explaining that what is in our self-interest is what brings us happiness and that this correlation with our happiness is the basis for what we call 'good' and 'evil'. In this passage it is not clear what "most" is meant to include and exclude. Either his claim is that *rational* people act in accordance with the principle of self-interest and that *most* people are rational; or that *most* rational people act in this way but that other rational ways of acting are also possible. Since the conclusion in (3) states that "every reasonable man ought so to frame his actions as that they may most effectually contribute to promote his eternal interest" and the conclusion in (4) covers "every man who acts up to the principles of reason", this strongly suggests that Berkeley has the former view in mind. Berkeley also seems to imply this in a famous statement made some years earlier in his *Notebooks*: "I never blame a man for acting upon interest. He's a *fool* who acts upon any other principles" (§542, my italics).

In (2) he explains that at the start of our lives we identify sensible pleasure and pain with good and evil. However, by gathering and analysing experience and by the emergence of our "nobler faculties" we depart from this simple sense-hedonic view in two ways. First, we come to adjust our reasoning in accordance with the realization that a smaller amount of present pleasure is sometimes followed by a greater pain at a later moment in time, and vice versa. Second, we come to appreciate non-sensible pleasures (such as the arts, see *Notebook* §852) and in fact recognize them as of greater value to our happiness than sensible pleasures. The temporal point is then brought to bear on (3), where Berkeley distinguishes between finite self-interest and infinite self-interest. He argues that since greater future happiness outweighs lesser present happiness, so infinite future happiness outweighs any amount of present and future finite happiness. Then, in (4) he states that God exists and that he can make us forever happy or miserable and that for this reason, following the will of God is the only rule that should govern a rational person's moral actions. This theological hedonistic account of 'good' was common at the time and is found also in Locke's *Essay* (2.20.2, 2.21.42, 2.28.5).

On the basis of (1) can see that Berkeley takes human psychology to be structured in such a way that we are only able to act on what we find to be in our interest to do, or what we are motivated to do. Accordingly, what counts as a reason for us to act must be something that fits with our internal objectives. This view is commonly known as 'reason internalism'. Given Berkeley's doctrine of the 'language of nature' we can see how the laws of pain and pleasure allows us to regulate our actions in a rational way. We are intrinsically motivated to avoid pain and seek pleasure, since the world is a hedonic nexus (as so-called primary qualities are assimilated with so-called secondary qualities, which in final analysis are understood as degrees of pain and pleasure), which God allows us to navigate by setting up regularities between visual and tactile ideas. This allows us to understand a visual sensation (say, of an approaching car) as a sign of a tactile sensation (great pain) which allows us to step out of the way.

Stephen Darwall (2005: 322ff) has argued that the picture of human psychology that Berkeley presents in *Passive Obedience* strongly suggests that a central aspect of Berkeley's moral theory, his account of moral obligation, was based on his psychological theory of action, according to which we are morally obligated to do something if and only if we have internal reasons to act in that way. This can be characterized as a 'normative monism'. On this view God's prescription and law is an unfortunate third wheel. Yes, God has arranged things in such a way that what is good and what it is in our interest to do coheres, but since we do the things we do solely on the basis of our self-interested motives, God's law and command are normatively inefficient here.

What Berkeley says in the passage that immediately follows the text cited above is inconsistent with such a reductive account of obligation:

> The same conclusion doth likewise evidently result from the relation which God bears to his creatures. God alone is maker and preserver of all things. He is, therefore, with the most undoubted right, the great legislator of the world, and mankind are, by all the ties of duty, no less than interest, bound to obey His laws.
>
> (*Works* 6: 21)

Here Berkeley states that there are two "ties" by which we are "bound to obey" the moral law. In addition to self-interest, God as creator and preserver of the world has authority over his creations, and mankind is for this reason obliged to follow the law that the "great legislator of the world" has set. This source of obligation is itself external to our motives and issues from God's will. Therefore, Berkeley is stating that the ground for moral obligation is not exhausted by considerations of our internal reasons for action. Berkeley and a number of other early modern thinkers believed in order that a human being do anything, it is necessary that she has a motive to act. To that extent 'bindingness', 'obligation', 'normativity', in short, the 'ought to do' consists in internal reasons for action. However, when we move from the most abstract account of normativity to some particular form of action, it seems that something more might be necessary. For example, in order to say *anything,* I must have an internal reason to make an utterance. To say *something ironically*, I must make an utterance where I use language that normally signifies the opposite to express my meaning and do so, typically, for humorous or emphatic effect. To do that, I must understand various external, socially determined, linguistic rules and how to apply them and how to play with those rules in somewhat ambiguous ways. No one would dream of presenting a reductive account of irony in terms of internal reasons for action, should we do so for moral obligation?

In the next section Berkeley conducts an examination of the content of the moral law. Here his starting point is not our self-interest, but God's will.

> Hence we should above all things endeavour to trace out the Divine
> will, or the general design of Providence with regard to mankind, and
> the methods most directly tending to the accomplishment of that
> design, and this seems the genuine and proper way for discovering
> the laws of nature. For laws being rules directive of our actions to
> the end intended by the legislator, in order to attain the knowledge
> of God's laws, we ought first to inquire what that end is which He
> designs should be carried on by human actions.
>
> (*Works* 6: 19)

Because God is a rightful legislator, moral goodness will consist in
conformity with his will and law. As it is the nature of a law to direct
actions to the end intended by the legislator, the correct method for
discovering the moral law is to consider the intention and end that
God has for those (whoever they might be) whom the law aims to
direct and guide. This is in stark contrast to a metaphysical conception of morality that holds it to be reducible to human motives for
action. Berkeley continues:

> Now, as God is a being of infinite goodness, it is plain the end He pro-
> poses is good. But, God enjoying in Himself all possible perfection, it
> follows that it is not His own good, but that of His creatures. Again,
> the moral actions of men are entirely terminated within themselves,
> so as to have no influence on the other orders of intelligences or rea-
> sonable creatures; the end therefore to be procured by them can be no
> other than the good of men.
>
> (*Works* 6: 21)

In order to discover the content of God's law, Berkeley first notes
that God is infinitely good and therefore that the end to which the
law is directed is itself good. He further argues that as God has all
possible perfections, the end he has in sight is not his own good but
the good of his creatures. Berkeley continues by stating that human
moral action can only be evaluated within the sphere of human concerns, excluding all other thinking beings (such as animals) and so
the end that God wants humans to reach by means of the moral law
is the good of mankind. On Berkeley's view, the fact that the moral
law prescribes human good in not grounded in a consideration of *our*

motives for action. Rather it is founded on the 'motives' or 'intentions' of God as omnipotent and omniscient lawmaker, in so far as they concern his creatures. In Berkeley's words, "that end which [. . .] He designs should be carried on by human actions" (*Passive Obedience* 6:21). This coheres with the central aspects of the concept of a 'law', the idea that what is commanded by a law is necessarily something that its subject does not want to do by herself. As Locke expressed it, a "natural Convenience, or Inconvenience, would operate of it self without a Law" (Locke *Essay* 2.28.6) For this reason it is necessary that the law has annexed to it rewards and punishments that give the person of whom it demands something motives for acting in accordance with the law: "we must, where-ever we suppose a Law, suppose also some Reward or Punishment annexed to that Law" (Locke *Essay* 2.28.6).

The divine law then has precisely the structure of 'normative dualism'. One 'force' is that which God wills and codifies into law and it is necessarily external to our own interests, that is, external to the sense-hedonic system that is the sensible world. As no one would, of her own accord, follow such a law, there is, for this reason, necessarily a second, completely different and internal action-directing feature attached to the law, which makes it humanly rational to follow it. When Berkeley states "laws being rules directive of our actions to the end intended by the legislator" it is reasonable to take this to indicate that the moral law plays an irreducibly dual normative role. It is both "directive of our actions" and directive to "the end intended by the legislator". Within the classification used by moral philosophers this qualifies as a species of 'natural law' theory. Berkeley should then be understood as holding a 'conjunctive' view of moral obligation according to which there are two necessary and jointly sufficient conditions for moral obligation.

FURTHER READING

On the duality between mind and idea see David Berman, *Idealism and the Man* (Clarendon Press 1994), chapter 1; Talia Bettcher, *Berkeley's Philosophy of Spirit* (Continuum 2007), chapter 3; John Roberts, *A Metaphysics for the Mob: The Philosophy of George Berkeley* (2007), chapter 3; James Hill, "The active self and perception in Berkeley's

Three Dialogues" in Stefan Storrie (ed.), *Berkeley's Three Dialogues: New Essays* (Oxford University Press 2018), pp. 123–35.

For readings emphasizing the activity of mind in perception for Berkeley see Roberts (2007) and Hill (2018). For a generally pessimistic account of the coherence of Berkeley's theory of the self, see Charles McCracken, "Berkeley's notion of spirit" in Margaret Atherton (ed.), *The Empiricists: Critical Essays on Locke, Berkeley, and Hume* (Rowman & Littlefield 1999), pp. 145–52.

The only monograph on Berkeley's moral philosophy is Paul Olscamp, *The Moral Philosophy of George Berkeley* (Martinus Nijhoff 1970). For a more recent account of Berkeley's moral philosophy offering an 'internalist' reading of Berkeley on moral obligation see Stephen Darwall, "Berkeley's moral and political philosophy" in Kenneth Winkler (ed.), *The Cambridge Companion to Berkeley* (Cambridge University Press 2005), pp. 311–38. For a somewhat different view of Berkeley as moral egoist in his early work and tending more towards natural law in the latter, see Daniel Flage, *Berkeley* (Polity 2014), chapter 7. Sébastien Charles (ed.), *Berkeley Revisited: Moral, Social and Political Philosophy* (Voltaire Foundation 2015) offers a broad collection of papers on Berkeley's moral, social and political philosophy.

BIBLIOGRAPHY

Allen, Keith. 2016. *A Naive Realist Theory of Colour*. Oxford: Oxford University Press.

Arnauld, Antoine. 1990. *On True and False Ideas*. Trans. Stephen Gaukroger. Manchester: Manchester University Press.

Baxter, Donald L. M. 1997. Abstraction, inseparability, and identity. *Philosophy and Phenomenological Research*, 57 (2): 307–30.

Bayle, Pierre. 1734–8. *The Dictionary Historical and Critical of Mr. Peter Bayle*. 2nd ed. 5 vols. London: for D. Midwinter . . . and J. and R. Tonson.

Berkeley, George. 1948–57. *The Works of George Berkeley, Bishop of Cloyne*. Ed. A. A. Luce and T. E. Jessop, 9 vols. London: Thomas Nelson.

Berman, David. 1986. The Jacobitism of Berkeley's passive obedience. *Journal of the History of Ideas*, 47 (2): 309–19.

Berman, David. 1993. Introduction. In Berman, David (ed.), *George Berkeley: Alciphron in Focus*. London: Routledge, pp. 1–16.

Berman, David. 1994. *George Berkeley: Idealism and the Man*. Oxford: Clarendon Press.

Berman, David. 2005. Berkeley's life and works. In Kenneth Winkler (ed.), *The Cambridge Companion to Berkeley*. Cambridge: Cambridge University Press, pp. 13–33.

Berman, David. 2009. *A Manual of Experimental Philosophy*. Jeremy Pepyat Books.

Borges, J. L. 1970. *Labyrinths: Selected Stories and Other Writings*. Ed. D. A. Yates and J. E. Irby. Harmondsworth: Penguin Books.

Boyle, Robert. 1666. The origin of forms and qualities according to the corpuscular philosophy. In M. A. Stewart (ed.) (1979), *Selected Philosophical Papers of Robert Boyle*. Manchester: Manchester University Press.

Bracken, Harry McFarland. 1959. *The Early Reception of Berkeley's Immaterialism, 1710–1733*. The Hague: Martinus Nijhoff.

Browne, Peter. 1697. *A Letter in Answer to a Book Entitled Christianity Not Mysterious*. Dublin.

Cantor, G. N. 1983. *Theories of Light in Britain and Ireland, 1704–1840*, Manchester: Manchester University Press.

Cudworth, Ralph. 1837. *The True Intellectual System of the Universe*. Andover, MA: Gould & Newman.

Darwall, Stephen. 2005. Berkeley's moral and political philosophy. In Kenneth Winkler (ed.), *The Cambridge Companion to Berkeley*. Cambridge University Press, pp. 311–38.

Della Rocca, Michael. 1999. "If a body meet a body": Descartes on body–body causation. In Rocco J. Gennaro and Charles Huenemann (eds), *New Essays on the Rationalists*. Oxford: Oxford University Press, pp. 48–81.

Descartes, René. 1985–91. *The Philosophical Writings of Descartes*. Trans. John Cottingham, Robert Stoothoff, Dugald Murdoch and Anthony Kenny. 3 vols. Cambridge: Cambridge University Press.

Descartes, René. 1996. *Œuvres de Descartes*. Ed. Charles Adam and Paul Tannery. Nouvelle édition. 11 vols. Paris: J. Vrin.

Dicker, Georges. 2011. *Berkeley's Idealism: A Critical Examination*. Oxford: Oxford University Press.

Diogenes Laertius 1931. *Lives of Eminent Philosophers*, Vol. 2. Trans. R. D. Hicks. London: Harvard University Press.

Downing, Lisa. 2018. Sensible qualities and secondary qualities in the first dialogue. In Stefan Storrie (ed.), *Berkeley's Three Dialogues: New Essays*. Oxford: Oxford University Press, pp. 7–23.

Flage, Daniel. 2014. *Berkeley*. Cambridge: Polity.

Frankel, Melissa. 2013. Acts, ideas, and objects in Berkeley's metaphysics. *Canadian Journal of Philosophy*, 43 (4): 475–93.

Gallois, Andre. 1974. Berkeley's master argument. *Philosophical Review*, 83 (1): 55–69.

Garber, Daniel. 1993. Descartes and occasionalism. In Steven Nadler (ed.), *Causation in Early Modern Philosophy*. University Park: Pennsylvania State University Press, pp. 9–26.

Garber, Daniel. 2012. Descartes against the materialists. In K. Detlefsen (ed.), *Descartes' Meditations: A Critical Guide*. Cambridge: Cambridge University Press, pp. 45–63.

Hill, James. 2018. The active self and perception in Berkeley's *Three Dialogues*. In Stefan Storrie (ed.), *Berkeley's Three Dialogues: New Essays*. Oxford: Oxford University Press, pp. 123–35.

Hobbes, Thomas. 1652. *De corpore poltico, or The Elements of Law, Moral and Politick with Discourses upon Severall Heads*. London: T. R. for J. Ridely.

Jacovides, Michael. 1999. Locke's resemblance theses. *Philosophical Review*, 108 (4): 461–96.

Locke, John. 1975. *An Essay concerning Human Understanding*. Ed. P. H. Nidditch. Oxford: Clarendon Press.

Luce, Arthur A. 1949. *The Life of George Berkeley, Bishop of Cloyne*. London: Thomas Nelson.

Mackie, John L. 1976. *Problems from Locke*. Oxford: Clarendon Press.

Malebranche, Nicolas. 1997. *The Search after Truth*. Trans. and ed. T. M. Lennon and P. J. Olscamp. Cambridge: Cambridge University Press.

Malebranche, Nicolas. 1997. *Dialogues on Metaphysics and on Religion*. Tr. and ed. N. Jolley and D. Scott. Cambridge: Cambridge University Press.

Marušić, Jennifer Smalligan. 2018. Berkeley on the objects of perception. In Stefan Storrie (ed.), *Berkeley's Three Dialogues: New Essays*. Oxford: Oxford University Press, pp. 40–60.

McCracken, Charles, and Ian C. Tipton (eds). 2000. *Berkeley's* Principles *and* Dialogues: *Background Source Materials*. Cambridge: Cambridge University Press.

Muehlmann, Robert G. 1992. *Berkeley's Ontology*. Indianapolis: Hackett.

Pessin, Andrew. 2003. Descartes's nomic concurrentism: Finite causation and divine concurrence. *Journal of the History of Philosophy*, 41 (1): 25–49.

Pitcher, George. 1969. Minds and ideas in Berkeley. *American Philosophical Quarterly*, 6 (3): 198–207.

Popkin, Richard H. 1960. *The History of Scepticism from Erasmus to Descartes*. New York: Humanities Press.

Popkin, Richard H. 1979. Review of E. M. Curley, *Descartes against the Skeptics*. *International Studies in Philosophy*, 11: 218–20.

Popkin, Richard. 2003. *The History of Scepticism: From Savonarola to Bayle*. Oxford: Oxford University Press.

Rickless, Samuel. 2013. *Berkeley's Argument for Idealism*. Oxford: Oxford University Press.

Rickless, Samuel. 2018. Berkeley's argument for the existence of God in the *Three Dialogues*. In Stefan Storrie (ed.), *Berkeley's Three Dialogues: New Essays*. Oxford: Oxford University Press, pp. 84–105.

Ross, Ian Campbell. 2005. Was Berkeley a Jacobite? Passive obedience revisited. *Eighteenth-Century Ireland / Iris an Dá Chultúr*, 20: 17–30.

Schmaltz, Tad M. 2005. *Radical Cartesianism: The French Reception of Descartes*. Cambridge: Cambridge University Press.

Sextus Empiricus. 2000. *Outlines of Pyrrhonism*. London: Harvard University Press.

Stoneham, Tom. 2002. *Berkeley's World: An Examination of the Three Dialogues*. Oxford: Oxford University Press.

Stoneham, Tom. 2017. Three dialogues between Hylas, Philonous, and the sceptic. In Richard Brook and Bertil Belfrage (eds), *The Bloomsbury Companion to Berkeley*. London: Bloomsbury, pp. 121–40.

Storrie, Stefan. 2012. What is it the unbodied spirit cannot do? Berkeley and Barrow on the nature of geometrical construction. *British Journal for the History of Philosophy*, 20 (2): 249–68.

Storrie, Stefan. 2013. Kant's understanding of 'idealism' in the *Metaphysik Herder*: Idealism, solipsism and egoism. In Margit Ruffing, Claudio La Rocca, Alfredo Ferrarin and Stefano Bacin (eds), *Kant und die Philosophie in weltbürgerlicher Absicht: Akten des XI. Kant-Kongresses 2010*. Berlin: De Gruyter, pp. 509–18.

Storrie, Stefan. 2018. The scope of Berkeley's idealism in the 1734 edition of the *Three Dialogues*. In Stefan Storrie (ed.), *Berkeley's Three Dialogues: New Essays*. Oxford: Oxford University Press, pp. 160–75.

Stroud, Barry. 1980. Berkeley v. Locke on primary qualities. *Philosophy*, 55 (212): 149–66.

Taylor, C. C. W. 1978. Berkeley's theory of abstract ideas. *Philosophical Quarterly*, 28 (111): 97–115.

Toland, John. 1696. *Christianity Not Mysterious*. London.

Treisman, Anne and Garry Gelade. 1980. A feature-integration theory of attention. *Cognitive Psychology*, 12 (1): 97–136.

Treisman, Anne and Hilary Schmidt. 1982. Illusory conjunctions in the perception of objects. *Cognitive Psychology*, 14: 107–41.

Verberne Tom. 1976. Borges, Luria and hypermnesia: A note. *Australian & New Zealand Journal of Psychiatry*, 10 (3): 253–5.

Weinberg, Julius R. 1965. *Abstraction, Relation, and Induction*. Madison: University of Wisconsin Press.

Wilson, Margaret. 1982. Did Berkeley completely misunderstand the basis of the primary-secondary quality distinction in Locke? In *Berkeley: Critical and Interpretive Essays*. Minneapolis: University of Minnesota Press, pp. 108–24.

Wilson, Margaret. 1987. Berkeley on the mind-dependence of colors. *Pacific Philosophical Quarterly*, 68: 249–64.

Winkler, Kenneth P. 1985. Unperceived objects and Berkeley's denial of blind agency. *Hermathena*, 139: 81–100.

Winkler, Kenneth P. 1989. *Berkeley: An Interpretation*. Oxford: Clarendon Press.

Index